BULBS

FOR

INDOORS

YEAR-ROUND
WINDOWSILL
SPLENDOR

FOR THE ADVANCEMENT OF BOTANY AND THE SERVICE OF THE CITY

BROOKLYN BOTANIC GARDEN PUBLICATIONS
· MCMXCVI ·

Janet Marinelli
SERIES EDITOR

Beth Hanson
ASSOCIATE EDITOR

Bekka Lindstrom
ART DIRECTOR

Stephen K-M. Tim
VICE PRESIDENT, SCIENCE, LIBRARY & PUBLICATIONS

Judith D. Zuk
PRESIDENT

Elizabeth Scholtz
DIRECTOR EMERITUS

BULBS

FOR INDOORS

YEAR-ROUND WINDOWSILL SPLENDOR

Robert M. Hays & Janet Marinelli

Editors

Handbook #148

Copyright © Fall 1996 by the Brooklyn Botanic Garden, Inc.

Handbooks in the 21st-Century Gardening Series, formerly Plants & Gardens,
are published quarterly at 1000 Washington Ave., Brooklyn, NY 11225.

Subscription included in Brooklyn Botanic Garden subscribing membership dues ($35.00 per year).

ISSN # 0362-5850 ISBN # 0-945352-94-8

Printed by Science Press, a division of the Mack Printing Group

COVER PHOTO: NARCISSUS MINIMUS

Table of Contents

INTRODUCTION

Year-round
Windowsill Splendor

BY JANET MARINELLI

OME FEBRUARY, I've just about had it with winter. The gray skies, the bone-chilling cold, the dearth of foliage and flowers— they really start getting me down. A few years ago I found the perfect antidote. I began growing bulbs indoors. Now, even when a blizzard is raging outside, my rooms are anything but bleak. Bright red and yellow tulips, golden daffodils and fragrant hyacinths dispel the winter blahs. And they're a lot easier on the pocket-book than a Caribbean vacation!

Obviously I'm not the only one who's discovered the pleasures of forcing bulbs for winter blooms. Fall gardening catalogs are chock full of choices, from dainty snowdrops to stately lilies to quirky fritillarias. And you don't have to be a yankee like me to appreciate their charms. Even southerners can enjoy the blossoms of these same hardy bulbs, which would not survive outdoors in their gardens.

There's a certain poetic justice in the fact that bulbs help free us from the restrictions of *our* climates, because they've evolved to survive an astonishing array of adverse conditions in *theirs*. All bulbous plants, technically called geophytes by botanists, are able to store food in stems, modified leaves or roots. This allows them to overcome potential limits to their growth such as periods of extreme cold, extended drought or searing heat. They simply go dormant, "lying low" for a while until more favorable conditions return. Then they draw on the reserves of food they

It may be snowing outside, but if you grow bulbs indoors, your windowsill garden can vibrate with the reds, yellows, greens and blues of spring.

stored up during the previous growing season to send up new leaves and flowers.

I became so fond of these spunky plants that I moved on from forcing hardy bulbs for a head start on spring to growing tender bulbs from tropical and sub-tropical climes of South Africa, Central and South America and Asia. Some of these beauties—clivia and freesias, for example—mostly native to South Africa, bloom in winter. Others, such as achimenes, flower in summer. Some, like *Eucharis grandiflora*, the Amazon lily, begin blooming in the fall. Which means by carefully choosing both hardy and tender species and staggering forcing times, you can orchestrate an indoor succession of blooms longer than that of any herbaceous flower border.

Working with Bob Hays, Mark Fisher and Scott Canning, the Brooklyn Botanic Garden experts who put together the encyclopedias of hardy and tender bulbs that follow, has introduced me to a whole slew of new bulbs that I can't wait to try, like *Eucrosia bicolor*, with its orange tubular-shaped flowers with elegant long, protruding stamens.

To create a beautiful indoor bulb garden, all you need to do is to simulate the conditions in the plants' native habitats. And so this handbook begins with a look at bulbous plants—not only true bulbs but also corms, rhizomes and tubers—their native environments and life cycles. Additional chapters explain in detail both how to coax the glorious spring-flowering types to bloom ahead of schedule and how to grow the tender bulbs that actually do best indoors for most American gardeners. A comprehensive list of suppliers will help you get your hands on even the most hard-to-find bulbs.

You'll never regret being house-bound again.

By carefully choosing both hardy and tender species and staggering forcing times, you can orchestrate an indoor succession of bloom that will last and last.

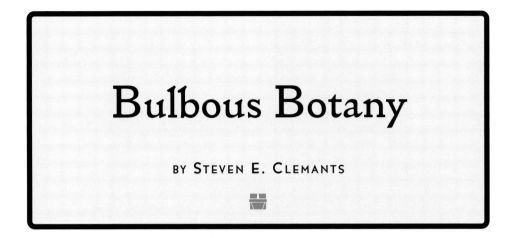

Bulbous Botany

BY STEVEN E. CLEMANTS

 OTANISTS ARE NOTORIOUS for changing the names of plants, but they are very precise about the use of descriptive terms such as *bulb*. To a gardener, a bulb is any perennial that overwinters as a fleshy, underground structure. To a botanist, bulb means something much more specific: a true bulb is a fleshy, underground bud. It is not a corm, rhizome, tuberous stem or tuberous root, all of which gardeners group together loosely as bulbs; these non-bulbs are in fact swollen roots or stems.

The botanical term for the gardener's bulb is "geophyte"—literally "earth-plant"—a term coined by Danish botanist Christien Raunkiaer. Raunkiaer devised a plant classification system based on where the dormant buds are located, and thus where new growth occurs. In geophytes, new growth begins below ground, while in other plants new growth occurs at or above ground level. In this chapter geophyte refers to the gardener's bulb and bulb refers to the botanist's true bulb. In other chapters, the term bulb will be used more loosely .

Like these calla lilies, seen here in their natural marshy habitat in South Africa, most geophytes are native to the so-called Mediterranean regions.

Geophytes like these *Homeria* and *Zantedeschia* have food reserves that enable them to endure harsh conditions, then bloom rapidly when the weather is right.

WHERE GEOPHYTES GROW

Geophytes come from almost every corner of the globe, but most of the ornamental species are native to the so-called Mediterranean regions. For example, alliums, irises and tulips come from the Mediterranean basin (extending east to Iran and eastern Turkey); *Camassia* and *Triteleia* are native to our own Pacific Northwest (from California to British Columbia); *Habranthus* comes from southern Chile; and *Agapanthus, Babiana* and *Boophane* come from southern Africa. A number of less frequently cultivated species are found in western and southern Australia. These areas, particularly the Mediterranean basin and California, have cool, wet winters, short springs and dry, hot summers. Geophytes can reproduce during short springs and survive long, dry summers, giving them a leg up in these climates.

11

BULB

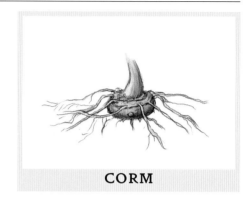

CORM

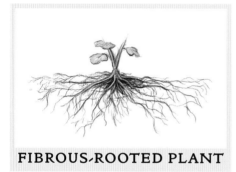

FIBROUS-ROOTED PLANT

Inside each hyacinth bulb is an embryonic flower waiting for the right conditions to blossom.

TYPES OF GEOPHYTES

It's a good idea to be able to distinguish the different types of geophytes from fibrous-rooted plants and from each other because this will help you determine how to plant them. One way to tell them apart is to group them according to where the starches and sugars used for food are stored.

BULBS

A true bulb is really just a typical shoot compressed into a shortened form. Food is stored in a number of small, fleshy "scale" leaves. Most bulbs are egg-shaped, with a stem "plate" at the wider end. Attached to this stem are the storage leaves, forming concentric circles surrounding the growing tip. (If you cut a bulb in two you'll see the concentric rings typical of an onion cut in half.) From the lower part of the stem new roots form, growing downward. So it's important to plant the bulb with this broader, root-forming

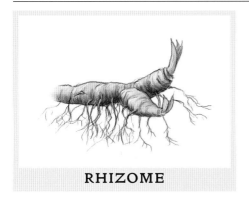

RHIZOME

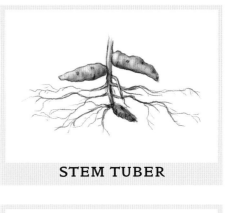

STEM TUBER

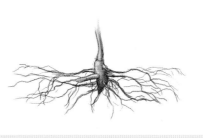

ROOT TUBER

end facing down toward the bottom of the pot.

Many of the commonly cultivated geophytes are bulbs, including tulips, alliums and lilies.

CORMS

In a corm, food is stored in stem tissue. Many corms look a lot like bulbs because they often have the same egg shape. But, unlike a bulb, if you cut a corm in half you'll see that it does not have the concentric rings of fleshy leaves. Instead, it is one mass of homogenous tissue—that is, stem. In both bulbs and corms, roots grow from the wider end, and therefore a corm should also be planted with the wide side facing down. Buds poke out of the pointy end.

Gladiolus, crocus and freesia are examples of corms.

RHIZOMES

In rhizomes, as in corms, food is

Gladioli corms, like crocus and freesia, consist of stem tissue acting as storage reservoirs.

Like corms, rhizomes are made of stem tissue, and are thick, fleshy or woody. As this ginger rhizome illustrates, growth starts anew at nodes or buds on rhizome ends.

stored in the stem. Indeed, a rhizome is a general term for a stem growing more or less horizontally below ground level. Thus you should plant it horizontally in a pot. Rhizomes tend to be thick, fleshy or woody, and bear nodes with scale or foliage leaves and buds. Growth occurs at the buds on the ends of the rhizome or nearby nodes. You can distinguish rhizomes from roots by the presence of scale leaves or the scars where old leaves have fallen off.

Irises, cannas and lily-of-the-valley are all rhizomes.

STEM TUBER

As the name implies, in these plants, like the two above, food is stored in the stem. It's often hard to tell a stem tuber from a rhizome; they're both swollen, horizontal, usually underground stems. But stem tubers usually form at the ends of a rhizome and will give rise to new rhizomes the following year. Growth starts from one or more nodes or buds called "eyes" at the base of the older stem. Like rhizomes, stem tubers should be planted horizontally in a pot, with at least one growing eye attached to each division.

The potato is the most easily recognized stem tuber, but some anemones and cannas produce them as well.

ROOT TUBER

Root tubers are swollen roots in which food is stored. Being roots, they lack nodes, leaf scars and buds. To be viable, they must include a portion of the stem with one or more buds. This portion of stem is usually planted facing upward.

Dahlias are the best-known root tubers; gloriosa lilies are also examples of this type of geophyte.

All geophytes, whether bulbs, corms, tubers or rhizomes, have a dormant period during which they shed their foliage and live off the stored reserves. The cyclamen tuber on the left is breaking dormancy with the sprouting of a flower bud.

THE LIFE CYCLES OF GEOPHYTES

You must understand a plant's life cycle to grow and care for it successfully. Armed with this knowledge, you will know when to water your plants, when to withhold water and when to repot and begin watering again to coax them back into bloom.

Geophytes, whether bulbs, corms, tubers or rhizomes, have one thing in common: they have a dormant period. During adverse weather—either hot and dry summers or cold and snowy winters—many geophytes shed their foliage and live off the nutrients they stored up during favorable conditions. "Dormant" is really a misnomer for this phase: though they appear to be resting, most geophytes continue to develop, but the changes take place out of sight, underground, fueled by food stored during the previous growing season. Geophytes are best transplanted at this time when they are not reliant on light or water.

When environmental conditions once again become more favorable for growth, the plant is stimulated to put out roots, leaves and flowers. Many geophytes adapted to cold respond to a rise in temperature; those adapted to hot and dry conditions are tuned to an increase in moisture. And

Many geophytes die after fruiting.

15

geophytes are tuned finely enough that they will usually not respond to just any rise in temperature or increase in moisture—a freak warm spell in December or a rain shower in July won't get a rise out of the properly conditioned geophyte. This mechanism protects them from sending out vulnerable shoots that will be killed off when more typical seasonal weather again prevails.

Geophytes often start their growing season with a rush, producing flowers and leaves at the same time or sometimes producing flowers before leaves. This effort usually exhausts the geophyte's store of nutrients and the plant either dies after fruiting or attempts to accumulate enough nutrients for the next flowering season. For this reason, you should not cut off the leaves after flowering; they are working to build up the food stores through photosynthesis.

Some dry-climate species (amaryllis, for example) may keep growing if you don't simulate the drought spell they would experience in their native habitats, but they probably will never produce flowers. Stop watering after the plant has had a chance to build up its food reserves, and let it rest for a few months.

PROPAGATING BULBOUS PLANTS

Many geophytes are easy to propagate. Bulbs and corms often form daughter bulbs (bulblets) or daughter corms (cormels) which you can simply cut off the parent and transplant. Often rhizomes and stem tubers only need to be cut into pieces, or divisions.

The most important thing to remember is that most new growth comes from buds, and so you need to make sure that each division or "propagule" includes a bud. To ensure successful propagation, learn where the buds are in each type of geophyte. In bulbs, for example, the bud is enclosed in the numerous scale leaves. In a corm the bud is opposite the broad end where the roots emerge. In rhizomes and stem tubers the buds are spread out along the length of the organ, and each is associated with a leaf scar, where the old leaf was once attached. In a root tuber the bud or buds are found on the small portion of stem at the top end.

Nerines and other true bulbs form bulblets that you can cut off and transplant.

HARDY BULBS

FOR

INDOORS

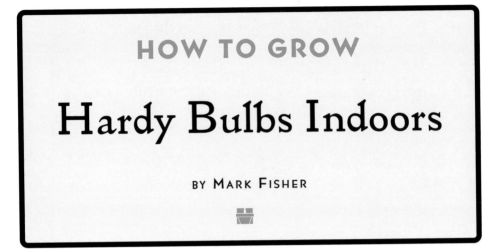

HOW TO GROW

Hardy Bulbs Indoors

BY MARK FISHER

AS EACH MARCH APPROACHES, I eagerly look for some early sign of spring. For me it is seeing the crocus push their way up through the partially frozen ground. I watch for them for days, until the one sunny day they burst into bloom and I know that spring is truly on its way. That day can seem to take forever, but with a little planning in the fall, you can enjoy a whole spring garden of colorful tulips, fragrant hyacinths and of course crocus—all indoors in February.

To get this spring bloom, you will need to "force" the bulbs. Standard forcing involves creating the conditions for hardy spring flowering bulbs—tulips, hyacinths, narcissus, crocus and other temperate zone bulbs—to flower when they wouldn't normally bloom. You can encourage them to do so by creating an abbreviated facsimile of their natural winter environment—cold. The cold that you supply will be of shorter duration than a natural fall and winter, but long enough to induce the bulb to send out roots.

Commercial bulb growers have been forcing hardy bulbs for many, many years, and forcing has evolved into an exact science with guidelines and schedules that ensure success. By applying the rules of this science, you can decide when you want the plants to bloom and work backward to determine when you should start the process.

Iris reticulata, a native of the Caucasus and Iran, is one of the most widely culti-vated of irises. Mix it with delicate daffodils in a spectacular pot, and you have a recipe for an unusual late winter flower show.

GETTING STARTED

To begin, select the flowers that you want on your windowsill to brighten your winter days. Choose named varieties that have been forced successfully over the years; these most likely will present the fewest problems. Among tulips, tradition-ally forced cultivars include 'Apricot Beauty', 'Christmas Marvel' (rose or red),

Choose varieties that have proven successful for forcing. Among hyacinths these include 'Pink Pearl', and a popular narcissus for indoors is 'Tête-à-Tête'.

While bulbs shouldn't be crowded into a pot, many look best in dense groups. In the right container, you should be able to plant ten to 12 crocus bulbs.

'Attila' (purple with a white edge), 'Paul Richter' (red), 'Page Polka' (pink with a white edge) and 'Golden Melody' and 'Hibernia' (white). Tried and true narcissus cultivars include 'Ice Follies' (white), 'February Gold' (yellow), 'Dutch Master' (yellow), 'Mount Hood' (white) and some of the shorter-growing cultivars like 'Tête-à-Tête' (yellow) and 'Jack Snipe' (white petals with a yellow trumpet). Almost all hyacinth cultivars force nicely, including 'Delft Blue', 'Ostara' (deep violet-blue), 'Pink Pearl', 'L'Innocence', (white) 'City of Haarlem' (yellow) and 'Hollyhock' (double pink). Among the best crocuses to try are Dutch hybrid cultivars such as 'Remembrance' (purple), 'Joan of Arc' (white) and 'Yellow Mammoth'.

When selecting any bulbs for forcing, look not only for tried and true cultivars but also for the largest, healthiest bulbs, and make sure they are firm, clean and unbruised. Tulips and hyacinths have a tunic, an outer paper-like covering that protects the bulb, which should be intact.

PLANTING

Next you will need containers, labels, planting media and a cool place to keep your bulbs during their cold treatment. Ideal containers are about 6 inches deep

GROWING BULBS HYDROPONICALLY

Hyacinths, crocus and narcissus are some of the easiest bulbs to force hydroponically—that is, using water as the planting medium instead of soil. Specially designed glass containers—hyacinth glasses—have an hourglass shape that will hold the bulbs above a reservoir of water. Any hyacinth cultivar, miniature narcissus, paperwhite narcissus and crocus cultivar will bloom if you grow it using this method.

Hyacinths can be purchased as "pre-treated," "pre-cooled" or sometimes "prepared" from mail-order catalogs. They've already undergone a partial cold treatment before they get to you. You'll need to continue the treatment, but your total forcing time will be three to four weeks shorter than with untreated bulbs. If you use several glasses and place them on your windowsills at weekly intervals, you can stagger your bloom over the long winter months.

Fill the glass with water to within ⅛ inch of the base of the bulb—don't let the water touch the bulb or it may rot. Place the bulb and glass in a dark, cool (40° to 48° F) location—an unheated garage or porch, basement or cabinet—for several weeks, and check the water level periodically, adding water as necessary. After four to five weeks you'll see roots emerging from the bulb.

If the water looks "dirty," change it by placing your fingers around the bulb and inverting the container to empty out the water. Don't let the bulb come out of the glass—you won't be able to get the roots back in. Then add fresh water.

In six to eight weeks, or even less, the bulb will sprout leaves. If you're growing hyacinths, you'll see the flower stalk emerging from the center of the bulb when the foliage is about two inches tall. When this stalk is about two-thirds of the way out of the bulb (1½ inches), put your plant in a sunny, cool (60° F) location. In a couple of days the leaves will green and the buds will start to show color, and in a week or so you will be

and 6 to 8 inches across, with holes in the bottom to allow for drainage. Each 6-inch pot will hold five tulips, four hyacinths, three to five narcissus (depending on the varieties), or ten to 12 crocus. Clay and plastic are the most popular materials for pots, but remember that clay pots will dry out faster than the plastic ones—and adequate moisture during the cold treatment is essential for success. If you choose to plant in clay pots, monitor the soil carefully, as it will need water

You can use almost any container with a small enough neck as a hyacinth glass.

enjoying the sweet smell of hyacinths.

If you're growing narcissus or crocus, put them in a sunny location when the stalk is an inch tall. Narcissus foliage won't get too tall and ungainly if you keep the plant in a cool (55° F), bright spot. In about two weeks, you can enjoy a sweet spring bouquet.

more often than if you use plastic.

Various potting media are available. The ideal forcing medium is well drained, yet able to hold enough moisture for adequate root production and to support the flowering bulbs. I use soil, sand and compost in equal parts.

Next, think ahead and decide when you want your flowers to bloom. If that's early February to mid-March, plant your bulbs from early October to mid-

As with all bulbs, make sure you choose the largest and healthiest crocus bulbs of the bunch. Plant them under about an inch of soil, chill for 15 weeks, and when the sprouts are 1 to 2 inches tall, bring them into a sunny, cool spot. Within a week or two, your work will pay off.

November to give them the 13 to 15 weeks of cold treatment hardy bulbs require to bloom. Plant them with their noses (tips) just above the soil level in the pot, or to about two-thirds their length. Tulip bulbs have a curved side and a flat side—not to be confused with the basal plate where the roots will emerge. Plant your tulip bulbs so that the flat side faces the outside of the pot. This assures that the plant will unfurl its first leaf toward the perimeter of the pot, and will have a fuller look. Cover crocus and grape hyacinth with no more than an inch of soil.

After planting, all bulbs need to be thoroughly watered. Remember to label each pot with the name of the cultivar you plant, the planting date and the date it should come into the house.

OUT IN THE COLD

Now place the bulbs where they will get a minimum of 13 to 15 weeks of 35° to 48° F cold. Some tulip and narcissus cultivars require an average of 17 weeks, but don't keep any bulbs in cold treatment for more than two weeks longer than maximum recommended cold time, as you will end up with flowers of poor quality. You're also likely to get low-quality flowers if you don't give bulbs the minimum cold treatment.

Look around your house for a spot that's sure to be cold throughout the winter—an unheated garage, patio or basement, for example. Old refrigerators can

When you bring your pots in from the cold, the stems of the plants will be color-less. Once in the sun, they will start photosynthesizing, green up, then bloom.

also work very well, but don't store any fruits—especially apples—in the refriger-ator with the bulbs, because the ethylene gas produced from the ripening fruit can cause the flowers to "blast," or develop improperly. Frost-free refrigerators can make the plants dry out quickly, so pay special attention to bulbs in modern fridges and make sure they have enough water.

For the next several weeks it is vital that you keep the soil evenly moist and watch the temperatures, because it's during this time that the bulbs are produc-ing roots. Without an adequate root system your plant won't develop properly

A profusion of spring blooms—tulips, daffodils, muscari, ipheion—looks stunning whether potted indoors or out.

and you're likely to get poor-quality flowers. Fully developed roots may take between four to eight weeks to grow—be patient. Bulbs root best at temperatures around 45° to 48° F. After a few weeks at this temperature, you may see roots by looking at the hole in the bottom of the pot. If the roots have grown down that far, it's a good indication that the bulbs are well established.

Once well rooted, bulbs prefer an even lower temperature for shoot development—38° to 42° F—the temperature range they experience outdoors. If your bulbs are in a controlled spot like a refrigerator or greenhouse, lower the temperature to within this range. In the northern tier of states, bulbs in an unheated garage or patio will also get enough cold. Your bulbs' emerging leaves will be white because they lack chlorophyll, but they'll green up when you bring them into the light. When the leaves of hyacinths, tulips and narcissus are 1 to 2 inches tall, or the sheaths of crocus and other minor bulbs are an inch tall, the plants are ready for forcing.

If they achieve the heights described above and are still growing but have not met their minimum cold requirement, put the bulbs in an even colder spot (33° to 35° F) for the duration. By 15 to 17 weeks the bulbs should be well rooted and have leaves about 1 to 2 inches tall.

For those seeking more instantaneous results, look for bulbs that have

Even after your bulbs have bloomed, they prefer a cool environment. At temperatures in the fifties, some will keep their blossoms for as long as 10 days.

By buying potted, pre-cooled bulbs, you can get instantaneous blooms.

been pre-cooled (mainly available through mail-order sources, see page 103); these will have gone through some variation of the cold treatment described above, depending on the bulb and the supplier. You should receive instructions from the nursery on how to proceed. Windowsill gardeners even more impatient will probably find potted bulbs ready to burst into bloom in late winter at their florist, farmer's market or supermarket.

FORCING YOUR WAY TO FLOWERS

Next comes the forcing. If you bring your plants in from the cold a few at a time, you can stretch the flowering season over many weeks. Bring the pots into the house and put them in a 55° to 60° F sunny area such as a windowsill or a table near a window where they will get at least eight hours of light but temperatures no higher than 60° F. Nighttime temperatures should stay within a 5° to 10° F range of daytime temperatures. Make sure your plants get enough moisture.

Because each bulb has everything it needs to produce its flowers, you shouldn't need to fertilize. After a couple of days in the sun, the leaves will have greened up and will start to grow. In two to three weeks, depending on the cultivar, your plants will bloom. The cooler the spot where you keep the plants, the longer the flowers will last—if you keep them at 50° to 55° F, some plants will keep their blooms for up to 10 days.

AFTER THE SHOW

Because of the energy plants expend during the forcing process, most bulbs (an exception is narcissus) are usually not strong enough to produce flowers the following year and gardeners often compost or discard them. To save the bulbs, add some low-nitrogen fertilizer to the soil immediately after flowering and weekly thereafter (follow the package directions) and keep the plants in a sunny location. The bulb can then build up the energy it will need to develop flowers the following year. When weather permits in the spring, plant the bulbs outdoors in the garden. Keep the foliage intact, as it will continue photosynthesizing. These bulbs won't be strong enough for another season of forcing but may do fine in the garden.

Encyclopedia
of
Hardy Bulbs
for
Indoors

Ornamental Onion

Allium, Latin for garlic, is native to the northern hemisphere from the temperate regions of Europe and Asia to the Middle East. Several species including onions and chives are grown for food. Allium flowers are blue, pink, yellow, white or purple, and arise from a single point in an umbel ranging from 2 to 10 inches in diameter. Over 700 species of allium have been identified, but only a handful are cultivated.

CULTIVARS & RELATED SPECIES:

Allium can reach 36 inches in height, but those no taller than 10 to 12 inches are best for indoor cultivation.

A. karataviense produces a 4- to 5-inch umbel of 100 pink-lilac, fragrant florets on a 10- to 12-inch stem. The attractive wide, dark green leaves are tinged with crimson.

A. moly has yellow flowers produced in a loose umbel on stems 8 to 10 inches tall. The foliage is long, narrow and blue-green.

GROWING TIPS:

Cold treatment: 21 weeks. Starting in the middle of October, plant the bulbs in a well-drained soil, three bulbs per 6-inch pot. Cover them with an inch of soil, water thoroughly and place in a dark, cool location. See pages 25-28 for detailed chilling instructions. After 21 weeks, move the pots to a 55° to 60° F location with the brightest light available. Keep them evenly moist and your plants will bloom in two to three weeks.

Allium neapolitanum

Windflower

Anemone is derived from the Greek word "anemos"—wind—the means by which the plants' seeds are dispersed. There are more than 120 species of anemone, tubers that give rise to blooms in shades of pink, red, blue and purple.

CULTIVARS & RELATED SPECIES:
A. blanda grows 4 inches tall and produces 1½ to 2-inch daisy-like flowers with a yellow center. Forceable cultivars include 'Blue Shades' and 'White Splendor'. *A. apennina* has blue daisy-like flowers and attractive foliage
continues on the next page

Anemone blanda

continued from previous page

resembling that of ferns.

A. coronaria, or florist's anemone, blooms on 8-inch stems. Unlike the species above, it does not require a cold treatment.

GROWING TIPS:

Cold treatment: 15 weeks. It's hard to know which way is "up" on anemone tubers—basically the shoots emerge from "eyes" on the top of the tuber. If you plant them upside down, don't worry, the shoots will adjust accordingly. Plant six to eight *A. blanda* bulbs per 6-inch pot in a 1:1:1 soil, sand and compost mix as soon as you get them because the tubers are very sensitive to water loss; if they dry out they may not flower properly. Water thoroughly and place in a dark, cool spot (41° F is optimal). After 15 weeks, move the pots to a sunny location; you may not see buds until then. Make sure that the maximum temperature does not exceed 53° F or your anemone will not bloom.

Soak *A. coronaria* bulbs for 24 hours, then plant them in a well-drained soil in a large container about 3 inches apart. *A. coronaria* doesn't require a cold treatment, so place the pots directly in a very sunny and cool location—they thrive in a greenhouse environment and need ample sunlight to flower.

Anemone coronaria 'Mona Lisa'

Quamash

Quamash is one of the Native American words for this plant, which served as a food for some native people; on their expeditions across the continent, explorers Lewis and Clark also ate quamash. This native plant of the mountains and prairies has long narrow leaves and six-petaled, star-shaped flowers in blue to white.

CULTIVARS & RELATED SPECIES:
Three species of quamash are cultivated: *C. cusickii* has narrow green leaves with light blue flowers on long spikes. It grows to a height of 20 inches.

C. quamash blooms a beautiful deep blue color and reaches a height of 16 inches. This is the species Native Americans consumed.

C. leichtlinii produces white, violet-purple and yellow flowers and grows to 28 inches tall. Notable cultivars: 'Flore Plena', with double sulfur-yellow flowers, 'Blue Danube' (dark blue), 'Alba' (white) and 'Semiplena' (creamy white).

GROWING TIPS:
Cold treatment: 15-17 weeks. Plant and chill camassia as you would other hardy bulbs (see pages 25-28 for detailed chilling instructions). At the end of the 15- to 17-week cold treatment, place the pots in a 60° to 65° F spot with plenty of sun. In three to four weeks your plants will come into bloom.

Camassia leichtlinii

Glory of the Snow

This little gem is native to Crete, Cyprus and Asia Minor, and includes five to six species of alpine or sub-alpine early-spring-flowering plants. Its flat, star-shaped flowers are held on short stems, less than 6 inches high. The flower stalk emerges from between a pair of narrow, dark green leaves, which die down shortly after flowering.

CULTIVARS & RELATED SPECIES:
C. luciliae, a 4-inch plant, produces a raceme of 1-inch light blue, white-eyed flowers. It is named for the wife of the Swiss botanist E. Bossier who discovered it in Asia Minor.
C. gigantea is a 4-inch plant with 1½-inch, pale blue, white-eyed flowers.

C. forbesii (C. siehei) produces up to 12 lavender-blue, white-eyed flowers.

GROWING TIPS
Cold treatment: 15 weeks. Plant six to eight bulbs per 6-inch pot in a well-drained soil. Cover them with a half inch of soil, water thoroughly and place in a dark, cool location. Keep the bulbs evenly moist throughout the cold treatment. See pages 25-28 for detailed chilling instructions. When 15 weeks of cold have elapsed, bring the pots into a cool 55° to 60° F, brightly lit room. In a few days the shoots will green up and in a couple of weeks they will be in full bloom.

Chionodoxa luciliae

Lily-of-the-valley

This European native with very fragrant, white, bell-shaped flowers grows from "pips" or shoots along a rhizome. Lily-of-the-valley produces two or three dark green leaves up to 8 inches long and 2 to 3 inches wide, and will reach a height of 10 to 12 inches.

CULTIVARS & RELATED SPECIES
'Flora Plena' has double white flowers. 'Rosea' has light pink flowers. 'Striata' has white flowers and leaves with a very thin white stripe.

GROWING TIPS
You can purchase prepared lily-of-the-valley pips—already precooled—from specialty catalogs. These pips generally require 100 additional days of chilling. Plant them 4 to 6 inches apart in a well-drained medium with the tips just under the soil surface. Water the pots thoroughly and put them in a cold spot. After 100 days, place them in a 60° to 65° F location, keeping them evenly moist. Because they're naturally shade-loving plants they don't need full sun to bloom, which they'll do in about four weeks. After they've finished blooming, plant them outside in the garden.

Variegated *Convallaria*

Crocus

Crocus derives its name from the Greek word "krokos" or saffron, also the name for the stigmas of one species, which are very colorful and important as a food colorant and flavoring. More than 100 species of crocus—a corm—exist. Some species flower several weeks or months before the silver-gray streaked foliage appears.

CULTIVARS & RELATED SPECIES

Almost all crocus cultivars can be forced, but the Dutch hybrids will perform best and will produce two or three large flowers per corm.

C. vernus, commonly known as Dutch Crocus, is the most cultivated of crocuses. Cultivars include 'Remembrance' (purple), 'Peter Pan' (pure white), 'Large Yellow' and 'Pickwick' (light lilac with narrow purple stripes).

C. chrysanthus, also known as snow crocus or botanical crocus, is often bicolored in a wide range of hues.

C. chrysanthus bulbs are often smaller than those of other species. Notable cultivars include 'Cream Beauty' and 'Blue Pearl'.

GROWING TIPS

Cold treatment: 15 weeks. Choose the largest corms for the best results. Plant eight to ten corms per 6-inch pot in a well-drained soil; cover them with about an inch of soil, water thoroughly and place in a dark, cool location. Check periodically to be sure the soil stays evenly moist. See pages 25-28 for detailed chilling instructions. When the cooling is complete, put pots in a sunny, cool (55° to 60° F) spot for two to three weeks, keeping the soil evenly moist. In a couple of days you'll see leaves emerge from the shoot and the flower bud in the center of the leaves, and in a few more days the flower will open.

Crocus sativus

Fritillaria

More than 100 species of fritillaria are native to North America, Europe, Asia and North Africa, but only a handful of these interesting bulbs are cultivated. Fritillaria species range in height from 10 to 36 inches. *Fritillaria meleagris* is the only species suitable for forcing.

CULTIVARS & RELATED SPECIES

Fritillaria meleagris, commonly known as snake head, guinea hen or checkered lily, can grow to 10 inches tall, has a slender stem with five or six narrow, bluish green leaves and drooping, bell shaped, 1¼ inch, pink-purple checkered flowers. The cultivar 'Aphrodite' is pure white.

GROWING TIPS

Cold treatment: 13 to 15 weeks. Time the forcing of your *Fritillaria meleagris* so that it blooms in February, not earlier, because it will grow better as the days lengthen. Fritillaria bulbs are sensitive to water loss—one of the reasons they can be difficult to force—so plant six to eight of these small bulbs per 6-inch pot in a well-drained soil as soon as you get them and keep the soil evenly moist so they don't dry out. Following a 41° F cold treatment, place them in a sunny 53° F location. If the room is any warmer, the flowers may fail to develop properly. The plant will bloom in about three weeks.

H
A
R
D
Y

Fritillaria meleagris

Snowdrop

This popular bulb, native to Europe and Asia, produces 6- to 8-inch plants with 1- to 1½-inch, six-petaled white flowers. Each flower has three long outer petals and three small inner petals, with green tips.

place the pots in a sunny, 55° to 60° F location, keeping the soil evenly moist, and in a couple of weeks the plants will flower. When they're done, plant the bulbs outside in the garden for bloom the following year.

CULTIVARS & RELATED SPECIES

G. nivalis, or common snow drop, is 4 inches tall with white flowers and narrow, flat, silver-gray leaves. Cultivar 'Flore Pleno' has double white flowers.

G. elwesii grows to 5 or 6 inches tall and has larger white flowers and broader leaves than *G. nivalis.*

GROWING TIPS

Cold treatment: 15 weeks. Plant eight to ten of these small bulbs per 6-inch pot in a well-drained soil, cover the bulbs with half an inch of soil and water thoroughly. See pages 25-28 for detailed chilling instructions. When the 15 weeks of cold have elapsed,

Galanthus elwesii 'Magnificum'

Dutch Hyacinth

Hyacinths have been cultivated since ancient Greek and Roman times and get their name from *Hyakinthos,* a Greek hero killed by Apollo. The scent of hyacinth blooms is one of the strongest of spring smells. This bulbous plant, native to Asia Minor and Syria, has bell-shaped flowers in numerous colors.

CULTIVARS & RELATED SPECIES

Many hyacinth cultivars are suitable for forcing, including 'Delft Blue' (deep blue), 'Ostara' (deep violet-blue), 'Amsterdam' (red), 'Hollyhock' (red double form), 'Pink Pearl', 'City of Haarlem' (yellow) and 'L'Innocence' (pure white).

GROWING TIPS

Cold treatment: 12 to 15 weeks. Some people develop an itchy reaction when they handle hyacinth bulbs. You can prevent this by soaking the bulbs in water for a few minutes before handling, or by wearing gloves. Buy the largest hyacinth bulbs you can find, and plant four bulbs per 6-inch pot in a well-drained soil, making sure that their "noses" are about three-fourths of an inch above the soil level. Water the pots thoroughly and place them in a dark cool location. See pages 25-28 for detailed chilling instructions. At the end of the cold treatment, place the pot in a cool (55° to 60° F) sunny location, and keep the soil evenly moist. You'll have flowers in two to three weeks.

Hyacinth 'Blue Star'

Spring Star Flower

Spring star flower, a member of the amaryllis family, is native to the eastern temperate regions of South America and is the only one of its species that is hardy. *Ipheion* is often listed under *Brodiaea* or *Triteleia,* but unlike these two genera, *Ipheion* is a true bulb. This onion-scented plant has a 1- to 1½-inch, star-shaped, six-petaled blue flower, which may have a slightly soapy odor.

CULTIVARS & RELATED SPECIES

I. uniflorum is a 5-inch plant with pale green leaves and blue-violet or white flowers. This is the *Ipheion* most commonly found in the trade, and it may be listed under *Brodiaea* or *Triteleia uniflora.*

'Rolf Fiedler' is dark blue.

'Wisley Blue' is deep violet-blue.

GROWING TIPS

Cold treatment: 10-12 weeks. In early to mid-September, plant five to seven bulbs in a 6-inch pot, in a potting medium that consists of three parts all-purpose potting mix and one part sand. Cover the bulbs with the soil mix, water thoroughly and place where they will receive 10 to 12 weeks of 35° to 40° F cold. Monitor the soil during this time, and keep the plants evenly moist. On completion of the cold period, put the pots in a sunny 55° to 60° F location. In about three weeks, the plants will come into bloom.

Ipheion 'Wisley Blue'

Iris

This genus consists of more than 200 species, and is divided into rhizomatous plants such as *Iris germanica,* the German iris, and the bulbous species of iris, which are grown as cut flowers. A couple of the latter are suitable for forcing.

CULTIVARS & RELATED SPECIES

I. reticulata, a native of the Caucasus and Iran, is one of the most widely cultivated of irises. The 5-inch-tall, narrow-leaved plants bloom in either dark blue, light blue or purple. Cultivars include 'Cantab' (sky blue) and 'Joyce' (deep violet-blue).

I. danfordiae, a native of Turkey, produces bright yellow flowers with small brown spots on 4-inch plants.

GROWING TIPS

Cold treatment: 15 weeks. Plant eight to ten bulbs in a 6-inch pot and cover with a half-inch of well-drained soil. Water thoroughly and place in a dark, cool location. Keep the soil evenly moist throughout the cold treatment. Then put your plants in a sunny 55° F location, and in two to three weeks your iris will be in full bloom.

Iris 'Mysterious'

Snowflake

Leucojum evolved from the Greek word *leicos*, "white ion." The snowflake, a native of Europe and the western Mediterranean, is often confused with the snow drop because it too has white bell-shaped flowers tinged with green, but *Leucojum* has a hollow flower stalk and produces leaves at the base of the plant.

CULTIVARS & RELATED SPECIES

L. aestivum ("of the summer") has three to five ½- to ¾-inch flowers on plants averaging 14 to 24 inches in height.
L. vernum ("of the spring") has five 1- to 2½-inch flowers on 4- to 8-inch-tall plants. This snowflake prefers a moist, organic soil.

GROWING TIPS

Cold treatment: 15 weeks. *Leucojum* bulbs produced in Israel tend to force more successfully than others. The flower develops gradually inside the bulb, and around the first part of October its development is complete, so don't plant the bulbs before mid-October. Plant *Leucojum* in a well-drained soil and cover with a half-inch of soil. Water thoroughly and place in a dark, cool location. When they've had the full cold treatment, bring the bulbs into a sunny 50° to 55° F location, and in two to three weeks the bulbs will come into bloom. You can plant them out in the garden and with proper care they will bloom again the following year.

Leucojum aestivum 'Gravetye Giant'

Lily

Lilies have appeared in works of art for hundreds of years, and come in an array of flower colors and shapes ranging from trumpets to Turk's caps to flat pendants to outward facing varieties. Many people consider them the queen of the perennial garden. While lilies are not difficult to force in controlled greenhouse conditions, the homeowner may find them a challenge.

CULTIVARS & RELATED SPECIES

Asiatic hybrids have upright-, outward- and downward-facing pendant flowers. Cultivars include 'Connecticut King' (yellow), 'Chinook' (pink with red markings) and 'Enchantment' (orange), and dozens more are available. Choose varieties that won't grow too tall—no more than 2 feet.

Oriental Hybrids, derived from the Japanese species *L. auratum* and *L. speciosum,* bear flowers that are large, fragrant and almost flat. They can average 4- to 6-feet tall.

GROWING TIPS

Cold treatment: Asiatic varieties— 6 weeks; Oriental hybrids—8 to 10 weeks. Use only prepared lily bulbs for forcing; these have been pre-cooled. Plant three bulbs per 6- to 8-inch pot in a well-drained potting mix, and at least 3 inches deep, as new feeder roots emerge along the underground stem. Keep the soil evenly moist and place the pot in a sunny location. When the shoot is 3 to 5 inches tall, the plant starts setting its flower buds, so keep the plant at 55° to 60° F in as much light as possible to allow more buds to develop. Lily growers control the height of their plants with growth regulators or a process called DIF, in which nighttime temperatures are kept 5° to 10° F higher than daytime temperatures. Lilies are heavy feeders and should be fed weekly with a well-balanced fertilizer. Aphids may attack your lilies; if they do, wash off the insects or spray with insecticidal soap or a summer horticultural oil.

Oriental hybrid lily 'Little Rascals'

Grape Hyacinth

Muscari is from the Greek word *moschos* or musk, the scent of some of the species. The flowers of this southwest Asian and Mediterranean native look like clusters of grapes and are borne on stalks 4 to 8 inches tall.

CULTIVARS & RELATED SPECIES

M. armeniacum is the common grape hyacinth best known for its blue flowers edged with white. Cultivars include 'Heavenly Blue' and 'Blue Spike'.

M. botryoides 'Album' closely resembles *M. armeniacum,* but has narrow and less compact bunches of white flowers.

M. comosum 'Plumosum', also called feather hyacinth, has mauve-lilac, double, plume-like flowers on 6-inch stems.

GROWING TIPS

Cold treatment: 15 weeks. Plant six to eight of these bulbs per 6-inch pot in a well-drained soil and cover with an inch of soil. Water thoroughly and place in a cool, dark location. See pages 25-28 for detailed chilling instructions. When the cold treatment is complete, bring the pots into a sunny 55° F location and keep evenly moist. In a few days the leaves will green up and you will see flowers emerge, then bloom. Grape hyacinths are great as cut flowers, too. After blooming, fertilize the plants and put them in the garden where they may bloom next year.

Muscari cultivar

Daffodil, Jonquil

The Greek myth behind the narcissus is the story of a youth of great beauty who was so entranced with his own looks that, as he gazed at his reflection in a pool, he was transformed by the gods into a flower. There are more than 26 species and 300 cultivars of this very popular bulb, which is native to Europe and North Africa. Flowers ranging from yellow and white to salmon are borne on stems 4 to 12 inches tall. Narcissi are made up of two parts: the trumpet, technically called the corona, and six flat petals that comprise the perianth.

Paperwhite narcissus

CULTIVARS & RELATED SPECIES

Narcissi are classified into 12 divisions based on the flower form. The following divisions include forceable cultivars.

The trumpet daffodils have trumpets the same size as the other flower parts and generally have only one flower per stem. Cultivars include 'Dutch Master' (golden yellow), 'Unsurpassable' (canary yellow with a gold trumpet) and 'Mount Hood' (ivory white).

Large-cup daffodils have a trumpet longer than the petals and produce one flower per stalk. Cultivars include 'Carlton' (canary yellow with a gold yellow cup) and 'Flower Record' (white to yellow with a red cup).

Short-cupped narcissi have a trumpet shorter than the petals. 'Barrett Browning' is white with a bright orange cup.

Cyclamineus narcissi resemble cyclamen, have a narrow trumpet with backward-pointing petals and come in both solitary and multiflowered types. Cultivars include 'February Gold' (gold to yellow), 'Jack Snipe' (ivory white with a yellow trumpet) and 'Tete-a-Tete' (lemon yellow).

Tazetta daffodils produce four to eight single or double flowers per stem and average 6 to 14 inches tall. Among this group are paperwhites,

continues on the next page

continued from previous page

which are not winter hardy and so don't require a cold treatment. Cultivars include 'Albus' (pure white), 'Grand Soleil d'Or' (golden yellow with an orange cup) and 'Cragford' (white petals with a vermilion-red cup).

GROWING TIPS

Narcissus tazetta doesn't need a cold treatment and will bloom four to six weeks after planting. Place three bulbs per 6-inch pot in well-drained soil or in a container at least 3 inches deep filled with pebbles. If you plant them in pebbles, make sure that the bottom of the bulb does not touch the water or the bulb will rot. After forcing, compost the bulbs or plant them outdoors for rebloom in zones 9 and 10. If planting in soil, cover the bulbs at least halfway with a well-drained potting mix; keep the soil evenly moist and place in a sunny, cool (60° to 65° F) window.

All other narcissus species require a 16- to 17-week cold treatment. Plant three of these large bulbs per 6-inch pot in a well-drained potting mix. Place the "noses" of the bulbs above the soil level, water thoroughly and place in a dark, cool location. See pages 25-28 for detailed chilling instructions. When chilling is complete, place the pots in a sunny 55° to 60° F location. If your room is too warm, the narcissus leaves will grow too long and fall over. After they've flowered, you can fertilize them with a low-nitrogen fertilizer, keep them growing as long as possible then plant in the garden. There's a good chance they will bloom the following year.

Narcissus 'April Tears'

Scilla, Squill

There are 80 to 90 species of scilla, African, European and Asian natives with six-petaled flowers ranging from intense violet-blue to pink to white.

CULTIVARS & RELATED SPECIES

Hyacinthoides hispanica, wood hyacinths, are native to Spain and Portugal. They bear blue, white or pink bell-shaped flowers on plants 8 to 10 inches tall. Cultivars include 'Blue Giant', 'Blue Queen' and 'Rose Queen'.

S. siberica, a hardy scilla, is native to Siberia and produces several beautiful blue flowers per stalk on 5-inch stems. Cultivars include 'Spring Beauty' (bright blue) and 'Alba' (white).

GROWING TIPS

Cold treatment: 15 weeks. Plant the bulbs an inch deep in a well-drained soil, and place in a dark, cool location. See pages 25-28 for detailed chilling instructions. After the cold treatment, move them to a sunny 55° to 60° F location, keeping the soil evenly moist. The plants will flower in two to three weeks.

Scilla siberica

Brodiaea

The genus *Brodiaea,* which has been renamed *Triteleia* by botanists, was named for Scottish botanist James Brodie. This North American corm produces an umbel of blue or white flowers on stems 14 to 16 inches tall. *T. laxa* is one of the few species that are commercially available.

CULTIVARS & RELATED SPECIES

'Queen Fabiola' produces a large umbel of intense blue-mauve six-petaled flowers about an inch across. The foliage tends to be narrow and sparse. This cultivar is the most commonly grown.

'Candida' has pure white flowers.

GROWING TIPS

Brodiaea can be difficult to force as it requires up to 16 hours of light daily. As soon as you get the corms, store them in a 68° to 73° F spot. In mid-October move them to a 48° F location for up to six weeks before planting them closely together in a well-drained soil in late November. Brodiaea then needs 16 hours of light per day in a 62° to 64° F location, and soil that is evenly moist. The plants will bloom in mid-April.

Triteleia laxa 'Queen Fabiola'

Tulip

During the 17th century, tulips were at the center of a mass hysteria that raged throughout Europe. People were so eager to own tulips that they spent as much as $300 for a single bulb. Today, the tulip is still the most important of all commercial bulbs: Holland exports billions of them worldwide every year. More than 3,000 cultivars now exist, the result of crossing cultivars and by cross-breeding species tulips with *Tulipa gesneriana*.

Species tulip *T. sylvestris*

CULTIVARS & RELATED SPECIES

Tulips are classified in 15 groups based on flower size and shape as well as time of bloom, number of petals and various crosses.

Single early tulips bloom on 8- to 12-inch stems. A few of the many cultivars include 'Apricot Beauty' (salmon pink with a slight fragrance), 'Bellona' (bright red) and 'Christmas Marvel' (deep pink).

Double early tulips are 8 to 12 inches tall, have more than six petals and are sometimes called peony-type tulips. Cultivars include 'Baby Doll' (yellow), 'Karcol' (deep gold yellow) and 'Stockholm' (bright red).

Double late tulips include 'Angelique' (pink with a white edge).

Triumph tulips are the result of crossbreeding between single early and single late tulips. They are 10 to 16 inches tall with strong stems. 'Attila' (purple-violet), 'Bing Crosby' (brilliant red), 'Golden Melody', 'Hibernia' (white) and 'Paul Richter' (bright red) are among those good for forcing.

continues on the next page

continued from previous page

Species tulips include *Tulipa bakeri* 'Lilac Wonder', which has small lilac-pink flowers, an orange-yellow heart and a white edge.

GROWING TIPS

Cold treatment: 15 to 16 weeks. Plant five bulbs per 6-inch pot in a well-drained soil, and plant so that the flat side of the bulb faces the pot. The first leaf that emerges will then face the outside of the pot. Add enough soil so that the "nose" of the bulb is above the soil level. Water thoroughly and place in a cool, dark location. See pages 25-28 for detailed chilling instructions. When the cold treatment is complete, move the tulips to a sunny 55° to 60° F room and if possible keep the nighttime temperatures within 5° F of the daytime temperatures. In two to three weeks, your tulips will bloom. Because they use a tremendous amount of energy to bloom indoors, they probably won't perform well in following years and should be composted.

Tulipa 'Flaming Parrot'

TENDER BULBS

FOR

INDOORS

Tender Bulbs Indoors

BY TOVAH MARTIN

IF YOU THINK THAT BULBS are solely a midwinter's affair, consider the caladium. If you're under the impression that bulbs are common little garden flowers potted off-season and given as Easter gifts, ponder the pleione. Beyond those majestic amaryllis that open their wide-faced flowers just in time for the holidays, beyond the sinningias that tug your heartstrings at supermarket check-out counters, all sorts of tender bulbs are available. Most hail from South Africa, a few come from South America or Asia, and they stagger their blooming performance and resting periods depending upon their individual cycles: some like it hot, some like it cold; some sprout in summer, some perform in winter. So, tender bulbs tend to be a little more challenging than your average 'Tete-a-Tete' narcissus. But that's part of their intrigue.

You probably never realized that many of your favorite indoor bloomers sprouted from bulbs. A clivia, for example, reveals scant evidence of its underground agenda. Its broad, strap-like leaves remain intact even when the plant is resting. Haemanthus and crinums are also discreet about their cycles. However, not all tender bulbs are equally apt to keep clothed throughout their dormancy. For example, some oxalis disappear totally from sight, not even leaving a telltale stubble as evidence of the once and future display.

Due to their diversity, due to the fact that they come from different habitats and have such divergent cycles, it's difficult to make rules that apply to all non-

You probably never realized that many of your favorite indoor bloomers sprouted from bulbs. A clivia, for example, reveals scant evidence of its underground agenda. Its broad, strap-like leaves remain intact even when the plant is dormant.

Curcuma rhizomes give curry its color.   *Globba* is a member of the ginger family.

hardy bulbs. However, those that flower in winter (mostly native to South Africa) tend to have some common denominators, while summer bloomers all share mutual preferences as to planting times. If you are sensitive to a bulb's cycle, you can guess its other wants and needs.

As a rule, both summer- and winter-blooming tender bulbs, unlike their hardy counterparts, should be treated more like the average pot plant. You can tuck a hardy hyacinth into a pot and provide it with scant light and little sustenance—it will perform nonetheless. Not so with the non-hardy bulbs. They must be given all the amenities that most houseplants demand, such as sufficient light, moderate water, a good rich soil underfoot and fertilizer during their growing season.

WHEN TO PLANT

The most immediate concern facing a gardener tackling tender bulbs is the planting procedure. In the best of all worlds, you would receive instructions with a newly purchased tender bulb making it clear exactly when it should be planted for peak performance. However, a goodly number of tender bulbs are exchanged among friends and might not come with any written information. In the absence of instructions, you'll have to look for clues. Winter-flowering bulbs (again, most-

Pleiones are native to Asia's woodlands.   *Kohleria* come from Central America.

ly South African) should be planted from late summer to autumn. Summer bloomers should go into the soil in late winter or early spring. Keep your eye peeled for telltale signs of growth—when the moment is ripe, shoots often sprout from the tips of tender bulbs before they ever hit soil. That not-so-subtle hint is your cue that the bulb in question is ready to be planted.

WHICH END IS UP?

There is one rule that all bulbs share in common. They all want to be planted with the growing tip facing upwards and the roots sinking down. It sounds simple, but you can't always easily discern which end is up. Tuberous begonias are particularly perplexing. Check for round, crater-like markings where the gone-by stem once sprouted: that's the top. Look for spiny vestiges of root growth: that's the bottom. The easiest bulb is achimenes—which is actually a rhizome and so can safely be laid on its side. When in doubt, make an educated guess and pray for the best.

GROWING MEDIUM

Tender bulbs are more particular about their growing medium than their

In summer, the odd, striking flowers of *Haemanthus,* the blood lily, resemble shaving- or paint-brushes.

From the South American species, breeders have developed begonias resembling camellias, roses and carnations.

hardy counterparts. You cannot just sink a veltheimia—or most other tender bulbs, for that matter—in sand or a forcing jar half filled with water. They require some oomph under foot. Most tender bulbs prefer a standard potting medium that is rich in organic matter but slightly sandy. To keep the bulb from rotting, good drainage is essential (the exception being calla lilies, *Zantedeschia*, which are aquatic). Clay pots are aesthetically pleasing and also provide ballast to keep the plants from tumbling over—especially veltheimias and agapanthus with their top-heavy growth.

HOW LOW SHOULD THEY GO?

Generally, tender bulbs are planted an inch below the soil. However, tuberous begonias typically should be only half-buried, while nerines, tulbaghias, crinums and veltheimias should be positioned so most of the bulb is exposed. It would probably do no harm to bury them, but it's certainly pleasing to see where the bulb spews forth its foliage.

Not all tender bulbs keep their foliage throughout their dormancy. This oxalis looks lush now, for example, but while it rests, it will disappear totally from sight, not even leaving a telltale stubble as evidence of the once and future display.

Hippeastrum 'Red Lion' before potting. The roots of these plants have been trimmed prior to shipping.

Plant amaryllis alone in pots about an inch larger in diameter than the bulb, with only one-third below the soil line.

WATER

After planting, water the soil lightly when it is dry to the touch (never soak the soil, especially before a bulb makes visible growth). Most bulbs prefer to be under- rather than over-watered. After all, the bulb itself is a water storage unit custom made to carry the plants over during dry times, and it can easily rot if too much moisture is provided.

LIVING QUARTERS

Because too much water can be detrimental, bulbs are best grown in tight quarters. In many cases, the pot need not be much larger than the circumference of the bulb itself. In fact, a rotund bowiea or veltheimia poking out of a cramped container looks quite fetching. Smaller bulbs such as lachenalias, oxalis, freesias, cyrtanthus, ranunculus, tulbaghias and achimenes should definitely be crowded several to one container. Larger bulbs should go solo.

Like many of the tender bulbs suitable for cultivation indoors, sparaxis is a cool-winter-growing South African native. It's easy to grow and a knockout.

LIGHT

You can leave the pot in indirect sun until sprouts appear, then place it in its permanent location. Most tender bulbs prefer bright light during their growing and blooming cycle. A south-facing window is ideal, especially during the winter when light levels are low. Oxalis and freesias are particularly uncompromising about their light demands. Most other tender bulbs will good-naturedly tolerate less-than-ideal conditions. Sinningias, cyclamen and clivias actually prefer the lower light levels available on an east- or west-facing sill. Achimenes are summer bloomers and are often displayed in hanging baskets on outdoor porches. If that's where you plan to grow them, be sure to select a shady porch protected from direct sun at all times of day. The same is true for caladiums, which frequently find a place in the outdoor garden. Zingibers can tolerate quite deep shade.

REST PERIOD

Although you should generally treat tender bulbs like the average houseplant, you must let them rest when the time is right. During a tender bulb's dormant period, stop watering the plant and remove it from direct sunlight. Winter-blooming bulbs require a summer respite, whereas summer-bloomers slumber in winter. Be sure to withhold water completely.

When to stop watering is not always clear. There's no question when oxalis, tuberous begonias, ranunculus, caladiums and achimenes are ready for dormancy: they send out no-nonsense signals such as browning up and dramatically dropping leaves. Not all tender bulbs drop their foliage and slip into a full-fledged sleep. Notably, cyclamen, eucharis, clivias, cyrtanthus, tulbaghias and zingibers retain their leaves while resting. No real harm would be done to these plants if you continued to water throughout the year. But you might not see blossoms. For example, clivias give no hint that they need a rest, but they refuse to set buds unless you withhold water between November and March.

When the foliage is completely dried with no sign whatsoever of growth, you can remove the bulbs from the soil and store them in a paper bag—not plastic bags, which tend to be damp inside. You can leave them in their containers—but only if you can resist the temptation to water the parched soil. Keep the plants in a cool, dark place while resting. Keep an eye out for the sprouts that indicate when planting time has arrived; if you don't furnish them with soil and sun post haste, growth will be leggy. Simply tuck them in the soil at the earliest possible moment. Then sit back and enjoy the growth cycle as it begins anew.

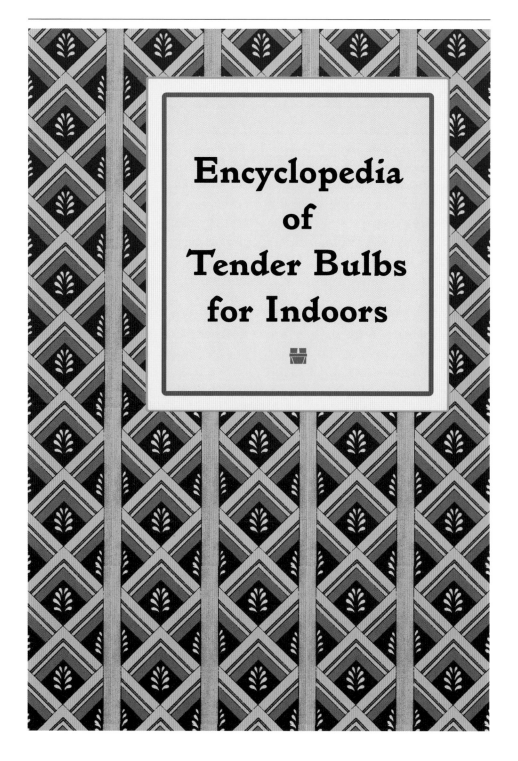

Encyclopedia
of
Tender Bulbs
for Indoors

Achimenes

Achimenes belongs to a small group of genera within the African Violet family that have scaly rhizomes. These rhizomes are actually small pieces of stem covered with closely spaced scales. Leaves and stems arise from the rhizomes and can reach a height of 6 to 24 inches depending on the species being grown.

Achimenes longiflora and its hybrids are among the more popular varieties grown. Native to Mexico, it can reach a height of 2 feet with an equal spread. The 1- to 2-inch flowers are borne singly in the axils of the leaves. Flower color is typically purple but can range from white, pink and blue to orange and orange-red.

CULTIVARS & RELATED SPECIES

Cultivars with white flowers include 'Ambroise Verschaffelt', 'Dainty Queen' and 'Margarita'.
Pink flowers: 'Adele Delahoute', 'Little Beauty' and 'Peach Blossom'.
Blue flowers: 'Galatea' and 'Valse Bleu'.
Orange/red flowers: 'Burnt Orange', 'Crimson Glory' and 'Master Ingram'.

GROWING TIPS

Summer and early fall flowering. Start achimenes anytime from February to May; by planting successive batches you can ensure a long season of bloom. Space rhizomes 1 to 2 inches apart in a shallow flat or pan and cover with a half-inch of peatmoss or vermiculite and water. Once growth has been initiated and plants are 1 to 2 inches tall, transplant them into their final container. Space them so that there are one to two plants per inch of pot diameter. Achimenes prefer rich, moist and well-drained soil and bright light shaded from hot afternoon sun. When blooming is finished, gradually dry off the rhizomes by withholding water.

Achimenes 'Desiree'

Agapanthus, Lily of the Nile

Oddly, this genus from the Cape Province of South Africa has nothing to do with the river Nile, but another common name of local usage, lily of the freeway, is easier to understand— masses of this plant grow in median strips and along highways in California. Its Latin name is derived from "agape," Greek for love. Globular clusters of blue flowers rise to 3 feet on bare stems above handsome strap-shaped foliage.

CULTIVARS & RELATED SPECIES

A. praecox 'Alba' is a white-flowered form that grows to 3 feet.

'Peter Pan' is a beautiful blue-flowered dwarf, growing only 14 to 20 inches tall. 'Rancho Dwarf' is a white-flowered dwarf, reaching 18 to 24 inches tall.

GROWING TIPS

Summer flowering. Agapanthus is an excellent container plant, attractive year-round and easy to grow. It prefers a moist and well-drained soil in full sun, but is not fussy. Feed it with a granular or liquid balanced fertilizer during active growth, spring into summer, and keep it slightly dry in winter. It can stand considerable crowding in its container but dividing may become necessary and is best done in early spring with a sharp spade or knife. The plant is largely trouble-free, but watch for slugs and snails, and if you overwater during humid weather, you may encourage fungus.

T
E
N
D
E
R

Agapanthus praecox

Shell-ginger

The genus *Alpinia* was named after Prosper Alpinus, an Italian botanist who died in 1617. Shell-gingers, which are native to Southeast Asia, are popular ornamentals worldwide in tropical gardens; the blooms are often used in leis. Outside the tropics they make fine pot plants.

Typically, these plants are tall, leafy-stemmed and herbaceous. In open ground, they grow to 12 feet, although they remain much smaller when cultivated in containers. Bell-shaped flowers—white on the exterior with a pale yellow interior—are borne in nodding racemes at the tips of the gracefully arching stems.

CULTIVARS & RELATED SPECIES

A. tricolor is a smaller species growing to 4½ feet. It has brightly colored, variegated foliage with yellow stripes originating at the midrib of the leaves and radiating out to the margin.

GROWING TIPS

Spring-summer flowering. Cultivation of shell-gingers is simple: start them into growth in spring. The plants prefer a fertile, moist soil and high humidity. They will remain evergreen if moisture is adequate; otherwise they will lose their leaves in winter and go dormant. Bright light is best; shell-gingers will tolerate more sun if given adequate moisture.

Alpinia speciosa

T E N D E R

64

Baboon flower

In its native southern Africa, this corm is a favorite food of grazing troops of baboons. The genus name comes from a latinization of the Dutch for baboon, *babiaan*. Compact plants up to 18 inches tall sport brilliantly colored flowers, usually bright blue but varying from cream to violet and crimson. Foliage is a heavily pleated fan of finely haired, lance-shaped leaves. Typically a winter-growing cool-greenhouse specimen, *Babiana* is dormant in summer.

CULTIVARS & RELATED SPECIES

B. pygmaea is, as its name suggests, a ground-hugging plant with surprisingly large 3-inch yellow flowers.

B. rubrocyanea, "Wine-cup Babiana," grows to 8 inches tall, with dark blue at the petal tops and crimson in the base of the cupped flower—very attractive.

GROWING TIPS

Late winter-early spring flowering. Excellent drainage is a must for *Babiana*. Plant in autumn in a soil mix containing no more than a third compost or prepared soilless mix; the remainder should be sharp or coarse sand with a bit of bonemeal. Grow in full sun with a daytime temperature of 60° to 65° F, and around 50° F at night. Water the plant carefully until its shoots are well under way, then water liberally during active growth and flowering. Fertilize lightly if at all; avoid nitrogen. As foliage ripens (yellows), withhold water and store dry during summer dormancy.

T
E
N
D
E
R

Babiana stricta

Tuberous Begonias

TENDER

Modern tuberous begonias offer spectacular flowers in a wide range of colors plus an exceptionally long season of bloom. From the original South American species breeders have developed flower forms that resemble camellias, roses and carnations, but often the beautiful flowers can't be mistaken for anything but begonias. An outstanding feature of tuberous begonias is their ability to put on a dazzling display of colorful flowers in the shade—which makes them especially adaptable to indoor culture.

Begonias have two different growth habits: upright and pendulous. Upright varieties can grow as tall as 2 feet and have thick, fleshy, brittle stems and huge outward-facing flowers. Pendulous, or "hanging basket," forms have more slender, lax and less brittle stems that display numerous flowers cascading luxuriantly.

CULTIVARS & RELATED SPECIES
Summer flowering. Beyond the very basic choice between upright or pendulous varieties, numerous types of tuberous begonias are available. The upright 'Nonstop' cultivars are reliable standbys with early and long bloom. Peruse the lush photographs in the finer garden catalogs to help you narrow your choices.

Tuberous begonia cultivar

GROWING TIPS

Begonias' cultural requirements are specific, but not difficult. Plant tubers in early spring to deliver a full season of bloom. Begonias require light, loose and most importantly free-draining soil. Many commercial mixes, particularly those with a coarse texture, are fine. Plant tubers very shallowly initially, hollow side up, and water with great caution until active growth begins. Make sure that water does not pool in the dish-like upper surface of the tuber. Start the tubers in flats or small pots because the tuber puts out roots from both its lower and upper surfaces. Repot at greater depth when shoots are 3 to 4 inches tall.

Grow your begonias in indirect but bright light with good air circulation. Begonias are moderate feeders, and prefer a balanced fertilizer such as a

15-15-15. Don't water to the point that the soil becomes waterlogged and don't let it dry out completely.

It you grow upright begonias, pinch back the stems to induce branching. Specimen plants are often staked and kept to one or a few stems. Begonia flowers occur in clusters of three, with a fully double showy male flower flanked by two, often single-petaled female flowers. If you remove the two female flowers, you'll divert energy to the remaining bud and optimize its size.

Transplant pendulous varieties into baskets when shoots are about 3 inches long; longer ones are more susceptible to damage when handling. Plant one to three tubers per container, depending on how big you want the finished basket to be. You probably won't have to pinch the plants, as pendulous types tend to be inherently freely branching. Make sure to thoroughly moisten the rooting medium when watering.

As temperatures drop in autumn, begonias begin dormancy. Quickly reduce watering, then withhold altogether. Lift the tubers from the containers and store them at moderate temperatures; many growers use vermiculite or coarse sawdust to cushion the tubers and to maintain a consistent, barely humid environment.

Begonia x *tuberhybrida*

Boophane

Boophane is a rare genus of bulbs from Africa cultivated for their showy flowers and unusual wavy foliage. *B. disticha* from South Africa, one of the two more common species, has been used to prepare poison arrows.

Bulbs of this species are large—up to 1 foot across. Usually only the tip of the bulb is apparent above the soil line. The foliage is thick and leathery, 1- to 2-feet in length and arranged in a single plane, like a wide-spreading fan.

Boophane flowers are borne atop 12-inch stalks in a head of up to 200 blooms. Flower color ranges from deep pink to red.

GROWING TIPS
Summer flowering. Cultivation is fairly simple. Start the plants into growth in spring. All they need is a rich, well-drained soil and full sun. When growth begins, soak the soil and keep it evenly moist throughout the growing season. With the onset of dormancy, signaled by the withering foliage, withhold water until the following spring. Repotting is only necessary every few years.

CULTIVARS & RELATED SPECIES
B. guttata, also from South Africa, bears purple flowers on 6-inch stalks. *B. haemanthoides* is similar to *B. disticha*, with yellow flowers.

Boophane disticha

Fancy-leaved Caladiums

This popular bulb native to Brazil is best known as a bedding plant for shade—it needs less light than most tender bulbs—but its use as a pot plant is increasing because it is both easy to grow and its highly decorative heart- or strap-shaped leaves come in myriad patterns of pink, red, green and white. It's often grown for a colorful foliage effect in spring or summer; its flowers are typical of the arum family and are generally insignificant.

CULTIVARS & RELATED SPECIES

Many caladium cultivars are available, and while the dwarf types and those with strap-shaped leaves are better suited for pot culture, you can grow any attractive type.

GROWING TIPS

Caladiums resent temperatures below 55° F both when growing and in dormancy. They are best started in late winter or spring when you will more easily be able to maintain warm temperatures. Three to five bulbs in a 6-inch pot is about right; use a rich, moisture-retentive but not soggy mix. Gentle bottom heat helps break dormancy. Liquid feeding is helpful, but only after the plant is well-rooted. Avoid drying conditions and direct sun. In the fall, when the foliage begins to decline, withhold water. When the plants are fully dormant, remove them from pots and overwinter in a warm location in barely moist peat.

Caladium 'White Queen'

T
E
N
D
E
R

Clivia

Clivia, an excellent container plant from South Africa, grows well in low to moderate light. Its 16- to 20-inch tall flower stalk supports a group of trumpet-shaped, bright orange to nearly red flowers, some with a yellow throat. Its handsome strap-shaped, glossy leaves are evergreen. The recent introduction of a yellow clivia has set off a wave of acquisitiveness not unlike "tulipmania," or perhaps the "orchid craze" of the nineteenth century. The rarity of this yellow form has yielded prices both newsworthy and outrageous.

CULTIVARS & RELATED SPECIES

C. miniata var. *citrina* is the much sought-after yellow form.

C. nobilis has pendulous tubular flowers that are orange with green tips.

GROWING TIPS

Late winter-spring flowering. Clivia flowers best when it is potted tightly and allowed to remain in its container for years. It requires excellent drainage and tends to be top-heavy when properly underpotted; for these two reasons, use a terra-cotta pot. Clivia likes regular, controlled watering in summer and minimal wetting of its leaves; keep water out of the crown of the plant to avoid rotting. Cool, 50° to 65° F temperatures and sparse water are its regimen for the fall; increase its water when the flower spike is initiated with renewed growth in winter. Clivia flowers better when it is "hungry" rather than overfed: feed it occasionally and lightly with high potassium food. Don't expose it to harsh sunlight. It's generally pest-free.

Clivia miniata

Crinum-lily, Milk-and-wine-lily

There are 100 species or more of tender bulbs in the genus *Crinum*. Their flowers are usually trumpet-shaped, although many species bear flowers with long, thin petals that result in a "spidery" appearance. Flowers are generally white but sometimes pink. Flowers arise on leafless stalks from late winter into summer and fall.

Crinum leaves are strap-shaped or broadly ovate and range in length from 12 inches to several feet, depending on the species. Some species are evergreen, some deciduous.

CULTIVARS & RELATED SPECIES

C. asiaticum bears fragrant, spidery, pure white and occasionally pink flowers in clusters of 20 or more. Foliage is evergreen.

C. bulbispermum, a South African species, is the most widely cultivated crinum in this country. Its bell-shaped flowers are borne in clusters of eight to 15. Flower color is white to pink with a rose-pink stripe down the center of each petal. Foliage is deciduous.

C. moorei, another native of South Africa, bears exceedingly fragrant, pale to dark pink and occasionally white flowers. Foliage is deciduous.

C. x *powellii* generally has pink flowers.

GROWING TIPS

Summer-fall flowering. Cultivation of most crinums is simple: all the plants need is fertile soil and adequate moisture. Water them freely throughout the growing season. Plants do best when left undisturbed in their pots for several seasons. Divide and repot only when necessary as growth begins in spring. In the fall after flowering, cut back on water but don't let the plants dry completely. Crinums do best in bright light shaded from hot sun.

T
E
N
D
E
R

Crinum cultivar

Turmeric

Curcuma is a genus of more than fifty species occurring from India and Malaya to Australia. Plants in the genus produce cone-like flower heads made up of bracts from which the short-lived flowers arise—individual flowers last only for a matter of hours but are borne in succession. Flower color ranges from white and yellow to pink and purple. Leaves arise from thick, fleshy rhizomes, which in some species are edible. Leaves are paddle-shaped; size varies with the species. All curcumas lose their leaves in winter.

Curcuma longa, or turmeric, is by far the most commonly grown. In addition to its showy cones, this species has been cultivated for centuries for its rhizomes, which are used to make curry powder and give rice and other foods that unmistakable yellow color.

CULTIVARS & RELATED SPECIES

C. petiolata is a species with yellow flowers. The upper bracts are purplish brown and the lower ones are green. *C. roscoeana* has yellow-orange bracts.

Curcuma petiolata

GROWING TIPS

Summer flowering. Cultivation of all *Curcuma* species is fairly simple. They do best in a rich, moist, well-drained soil in bright light shaded from the hot afternoon sun. They also prefer high temperatures and high humidity. In late fall when the foliage begins to yellow, you'll know that the plants are about to go dormant for the winter. During dormancy they should be kept nearly dry; resume watering, which will commence new growth, in spring. Repot and divide, when necessary, at this time as well.

Florist's Cyclamen

Florist's cyclamen, *C. persicum*, is the best known species in this genus, which includes at least a dozen others mostly native to the Mediterranean, Asia and Europe. Florist's cylamen has the largest flowers but otherwise is similar in appearance to other cylamen.

Cyclamen flowers are quite unusual, with large, upturned twisted petals and color ranging from white and pink to purple and red. The flowers, which are borne singly and held well above the foliage, bloom for several months.

Colorful foliage is another attrac-tion. Leaves are heart or kidney shaped and have beautiful silver mark-ings and mottling.

CULTIVARS & RELATED SPECIES

'Junior' Series is notable for its com-pact habit; plants reach 6 to 8 inches in height with a spread of 5 inches. Flow-ers are salmon, rose, scarlet or white. 'Concerto' Series comes in the entire range of cyclamen flower colors. Plants reach 10 to 12 inches in height with a 12- to 15-inch spread.

GROWING TIPS

Winter-spring flowering. Cultiva-tion of florist's cyclamen can be challenging; gardeners are usu-ally advised to discard the plants after flowering rather than trying to store and restart them. Start new plants from seed 12 to 14 months before you need bloom-ing-size plants.

Temperature is critical—50° to 55° F is ideal. Higher tempera-tures make the plants vulnerable to insect and disease problems. Plants require a humid environ-ment and bright light.

To regrow the corms, gradual-ly reduce watering after flower-ing has finished until foliage has withered completely. Store dry in the pots until August, then repot the tubers in fresh soil.

Cyclamen persicum

TENDER

Ifafa Lily, Vallota

This easy-to-grow South African native has graceful tubular flowers curving downward from the top of an 8- to 12-inch stem. The flowers have flaring mouths and a sweet scent and come in pastel shades of pink, yellow and orange. *Cyrtanthus* blooms sporadically through spring and summer, with a large flush in late fall.

CULTIVARS & RELATED SPECIES

C. mackenii var. *cooperi* is a recommended yellow form.

C. elatus, long known as *Vallota speciosa,* is still sold under that name; it's also called George-lily and Scarborough-lily. The plant is 14 to 18 inches tall and summer blooming with wide, trumpet-shaped, scarlet flowers.

C. obliquus is an uncommon but striking species with red flowers flaring to yellow. Plant with top half of bulb exposed in free-draining sandy soil.

GROWING TIPS

Spring-fall flowering. Plant five or six bulbs just below the soil surface in a 6-inch pot in spring for a good display in the fall. Use a moisture-retentive mix with good drainage and grow in full sun. Provide your plant with adequate moisture at all times—generous during summer's growth and a bit sparing during its winter rest. It will benefit from light liquid feedings in summer. Grow the plants in a cool spot in the autumn, with nighttime temperatures in the 50°s F for best bloom.

Cyrtanthus obliquus

T
E
N
D
E
R

Amazon Lily

In Victorian times these sweetly scented virgin-white flowers were nearly as popular as orchids for corsages. Unusual large, white, very fragrant flowers have a central "cup" reminiscent of narcissus, and grow several per stem above wide, deep green, glossy leaves. This evergreen bulb native to the South American tropics requires higher temperatures than most tender bulbs, recommending it to the warmer home or greenhouse.

CULTIVARS & RELATED SPECIES
E. x *grandiflora* var. *fragrans* is an especially sweetly scented form.
E. candida is a slightly larger summer-blooming species.

GROWING TIPS
Fall-late winter flowering. For the best appearance, plant multiple bulbs—five or six—per 10- to 12-inch pot, with the neck of each bulb even with the top of the soil. Use a very rich, moisture-retentive soil and grow in a warm room: nighttime temperatures should stay above 60° F. Once the plants are established, feed them moderately and don't let them dry out. Topdress the pots in spring with fresh compost, but avoid disturbing the roots. If you follow these practices, your *Eucharis* can thrive for years. Watch for mealybugs.

T
E
N
D
E
R

Eucharis x *grandiflora*

Eucrosia

This is a small genus of tropical deciduous bulbs native to Peru and Ecuador. The name comes from the Greek *eu*, meaning good, and *krosos*, meaning fringe, referring to the unique bloom structure.

Leaves of these plants are deciduous, shaped like paddles and 6 to 12 inches in length. Flowers are tubular, with six petals, and have unique long, protruding stamens. Blooms are pendulous and borne on stalks from 12 to 36 inches in height.

Eucrosia bicolor is the most common species—although even this is far from common. It's also one of the smaller species, with leaves 6 to 8 inches long. Leaves drop in late fall and do not reappear until after flowering occurs in the spring. The flowers are orange with greenish stamens and are borne in clusters atop 12- to 15-inch stems.

CULTIVARS & RELATED SPECIES

The four species of *Eucrosia* are generally similar, with variations in leaf size and flower color. All are deciduous.

GROWING TIPS

Spring flowering. Cultivation of eucrosias is similar to that of amaryllis hybrids. Soil should be rich, well-drained and kept moist during the growing season. Plants do best when left undisturbed in their pots for several seasons—divide and repot only when necessary as growth begins in spring. As foliage dies off in fall, allow the plants to become nearly dry until growth resumes in late winter. During the growing season, plants thrive in bright light shaded from hot sun.

Eucrosia bicolor

Freesia

Once famous for their scent, freesias, like roses, have undergone extensive hybridizing. Growers have selected for large or double flowers and strong, wiry stems. In the process the intoxicating scent has disappeared from some named varieties, while some hybrids retain the typical sweet to spicy fragrance. Keep this in mind when selecting from among the many cultivars available. If for you fragrance is more important than flamboyance, choose from among the species, which are native to South Africa.

Freesia hybrid

These are excellent container plants for cooler conditions.

CULTIVARS & RELATED SPECIES
Freesia hybrids come in a multitude of colors—blue: 'Amadeus', 'Blue Navy'; pink: 'Bloemfontein', 'Rosalinde'; yellow: 'Golden Crown', 'Riande'; red: 'Figaro', 'Volcano', 'Washington'; orange-red: 'Oberon'; white: 'Athene', 'Vienna'.

GROWING TIPS
Winter blooming. In September plant five to seven corms 2 inches deep in a 6-inch pot. Use a rich, moisture-retentive yet free-draining soil mix, and do not allow soil to dry out while the plant is growing! Place in full sun but keep cool; 60° to 65°F days with 50°s at night is ideal. Lightly feed with a 10-30-20 type fertilizer. Plants may need stake or ring supports while spiking and flowering. Continue to water and feed after bloom until mid to late spring; reduce water as foliage ripens. Store the corms dry during summer dormancy. Watch for aphids, spider mites and thrips.

T
E
N
D
E
R

Cape Gladiolus

Don't let your preconceived notions about "glads" mislead you, because you may overlook a delicate and delightful container plant. A number of species in this South African genus possess a refinement that recommends them over garden-variety hybrids for indoor growing. Several of the winter-growing kinds are ideal for pots: at 1 to 2½ feet tall they are a manageable size, and have delicate, sometimes fragrant flowers.

CULTIVARS & RELATED SPECIES

G. aureus has rich golden yellow blossoms; the plant is slender in all parts and grows to 2 feet.

G. carneus, "painted ladies," are white to rose with chevrons and blotches on the lower petals.

G. orchidiflorus has very fragrant, hooded flowers of a smoky pale purple suffused with green.

GROWING TIPS

Winter-spring flowering. Plant in early autumn in a deep container—seven to ten corms per 8-inch pot is about right. Use a very lean sandy or gritty mix with perfect drainage; you can add some bonemeal. Place in full sun with daytime temperatures in the 60°s F, the 50°s at night. Water sparingly until shoots emerge, then generously but only when soil approaches dryness. Fertilize very lightly, avoiding high-nitrogen formulas. After bloom, continue this regimen until foliage ripens. When a third of the leaf has yellowed back from the tip, withhold water, then store the plants dry in their containers. If overcrowded, unpot in late summer, and store in vermiculite until planting time. Watch for aphids, mites and thrips; too much heat and moisture may encourage rot.

Gladiolus colvillei

78

Globba

Among the ginger family, *Zingiber-aceae,* the genus *Globba* is little-known. Primarily understory plants in rich woodlands, most of the species are native to Indomalaysia and southern China. Only a handful of species are cultivated, but their flower structure has an unusual feature. The flowers are borne in arching or pendent racemes. At the base of the raceme, in the place of flowers, appear small bulbils, which can be used to propagate additional plants.

Globba winitii is probably the most readily available species. The flowers are borne in drooping panicles up to 6 inches in length. The golden yellow blooms are lined with showy purple bracts 1 to 1½ inches long, from which the flowers originate.

CULTIVARS & RELATED SPECIES
G. marantina has yellow flowers. Flower color of other globbas ranges from white, yellow and orange to purple.

GROWING TIPS
Summer-fall flowering. Cultivation of all globbas is fairly simple. They do best in a rich, moist, well-drained soil in bright light, but will tolerate a wide range of soil types provided there is adequate moisture. Plants go dormant in winter as evidenced by the yellowing foliage in late fall. During dormancy they should be kept dry; resume watering in spring to commence new growth. This is also the time for repotting and division, when necessary.

Globba marantina

T
E
N
D
E
R

Blood Lily

T
E
N
D
E
R

The odd, striking flowers of the blood lily resemble shaving- or paint-brushes in summer. Reddish buds on spotted, leafless stems arise after heavy watering in mid- to late-summer, then bud "valves" open to reveal tightly clustered golden stamens atop red filaments. Fleshy, rounded leaves emerge later, persist through winter, and wither as summer approaches. This odd but charming plant is native to southern Africa.

Haemanthus coccineus

CULTIVARS & RELATED SPECIES

H. albiflos is an evergreen species with greenish white blooms topped by golden stamens. It requires careful but even watering year-round. Avoid full sun in midsummer.

GROWING TIPS

Winter or summer flowering. The best time to plant blood lily bulbs is in early summer when this briefly deciduous plant is dormant. As with most amaryllids, try not to damage the fleshy roots. Plant the neck of the bulb level with the surface of a well-drained soil, and grow in full sun. Water deeply but infrequently through winter, very sparingly in late spring and just enough through mid-summer to prevent total desiccation. Resume watering in August to initiate bloom. Feed with a fertilizer moderately low in nitrogen and high in potassium through winter into early spring. Watch for slugs and snails and guard against viral infections passed along by sucking insects or unclean tools.

Ginger-lily

This widely-cultivated genus includes about 50 species native mostly to the warmer parts of Asia. The genus name comes from the Greek *hedys*, meaning sweet, and *chion*, meaning snow, referring to the fragrant, pure white flowers of some species.

Hedychiums have fleshy, rhizomatous rootstocks from which the graceful reed-like stems arise. Species vary from 1½ to 12 feet in height; potted plants are much smaller. The 2- to 4-inch flowers are borne in large clusters at the tips of the stems and are surrounded by large bracts. Flower color ranges from pure white and pink to yellow, orange and red.

CULTIVARS & RELATED SPECIES

H. coccineum bears bright red flowers with pink stamens in 10-inch spikes.

H. coronarium has become widely naturalized in parts of tropical America. Its flowers are pure white, intensely fragrant and borne on 12-inch spikes. The plants reach 4 to 6 feet in height, less in containers.

H. flavescens is similar to *H. coronarium*. The flowers are creamy yellow and heavily fragrant.

H. gardnerianum, Kahili ginger-lily, is the hardiest of the species and produces pale yellow flowers with protruding red stamens.

GROWING TIPS

Summer-fall flowering. Cultivation of most hedychiums is relatively simple; all that is required is fertile soil and adequate moisture. Water ginger-lilies freely throughout the growing season. They'll tolerate a number of different exposures, although flowering increases with greater light. The plants benefit from a short forced dormancy in mid-winter; to initiate dormancy, gradually reduce water until the foliage withers. Begin watering again in 6 to 8 weeks.

Hedychium coccineum 'Honduras'

T
E
N
D
E
R

Amaryllis

Hippeastrums are among the most widely cultivated bulbs for indoors. Most gardeners know them by the name amaryllis (actually a separate genus), and so we will refer to hippeastrums as amaryllis here. The genus *Hippeastrum* includes about 75 species. Those most likely to be cultivated are the large-flowered hybrids that come in a wide range of colors.

Amaryllis leaves are long and strap-shaped, measuring anywhere from several inches long to several feet—

Hippeastrum 'Mary Lou'

but usually 2 feet for standard varieties. The plants shed their leaves when they go dormant in late fall, and dormancy ends in mid to late winter.

CULTIVARS & RELATED SPECIES

The following hybrids are recommended:

'Apple Blossom' bears large pink or white flowers.

'Charm', a miniature variety, produces orange flowers half the size of standard varieties.

'Cinderella' bears large, red blooms striped with white.

'Red Lion' produces large, bright red flowers.

'Lady Jane' bears large, double, pink flowers.

'Scarlet Baby' is a miniature with red flowers.

'White Christmas' produces large, pure white flowers.

GROWING TIPS

Winter-spring flowering. Cultivation is easy once you understand the principles involved. Generally, the bulbs come bareroot—actually *rootless* because the roots have been trimmed prior to shipping. Pot singly into containers 1 inch larger than the diameter of the bulb, with no more than a third of the bulb below the soil line. The planting medium should be moist, well-drained and rich in organic matter. When the bulb is in place, be sure to press the soil firmly to get rid of air pockets. Water thoroughly at this time. Then water sparingly until the bulb appears to be in active growth, at which time watering should be increased.

Flowering occurs within a few weeks of potting; generally the flowers come before the leaves. Once blooming is complete, the foliage will reach its mature size and remain that way until fall. After flowering, remove the bloom stalks to encourage the bulbs to store energy. During the growing season, give the plants as much sun as possible and fertilize them on a regular basis.

When fall comes the leaves should begin to wither naturally; if they do not, initiate a short forced dormancy by gradually reducing water until the foliage withers. Store the plants dry in their pots. Repot the bulbs in fresh soil and commence watering after eight to 12 weeks.

Many gardeners have a difficult time making amaryllis flower the second year. This is often due to the fact that the bulbs had their roots trimmed prior to shipping the first year. Unlike many temperate bulbs, which produce new roots each fall, the roots of amaryllis are permanent and are slow to grow back. But be patient: generally, by the third year plants have stored sufficient energy and begin blooming again.

T
E
N
D
E
R

Cape Tulp

A bright and colorful South African species, which like many others is winter-growing, deciduous and summer dormant. Typically just one very long leaf emerges from the corm; it resembles a 2-foot blade of grass with a gently curved tip. Salmon-colored flowers last just a few days, but are produced in such numbers that several are open at any one time, and the bloom period lasts for weeks. The flower is six-petaled and slightly cupped, not unlike some species tulips.

CULTIVARS &
RELATED SPECIES

H. comptonii has orange to salmon spoon-shaped petals and yellow at the center of the flower; the plant grows to 18 inches. *H. ochroleuca* is nearly identical to *H. collina,* with yellow flowers.

GROWING TIPS

Late winter-spring flowering. Best grown in cool greenhouse conditions in the northern hemisphere. Culture as you would *Gladiolus* species, page 78.

Homeria comptonii

Spider-lily, Basket Flower

The approximately thirty species of tender bulbs in the genus *Hymenocallis* can be divided into two groups: those that are evergreen and those that are deciduous. Flower parts of the evergreen types, known as spider-lilies, are not fused together and thus have a "spidery" appearance. The deciduous types, or basket flowers, have fused staminal cups similar to daffodils. The genus name comes from the Greek *hymen*, or membrane, and *kallos*, meaning beautiful. It refers to the fused part of the flower.

The leaves of *Hymenocallis* are strap-shaped or broadly ovate and range in length from 12 inches to sev-eral feet, depending on the species. With the exception of one species, which bears yellow flowers, *Hymenocallis* blooms are white and arise on leafless stalks directly from the bulbs. Flowering may occur anytime from late winter to summer, again depending on the species being grown.

CULTIVARS & RELATED SPECIES

H. caribaea is an evergreen species from the West Indies bearing flowers in a cluster of eight to 12 atop 12-inch stalks in late winter.

H. littoralis, a larger evergreen species from tropical America, produces four to 12 flowers on 1½- to 2½-foot stems.

continues on the next page

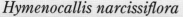

Hymenocallis narcissiflora

continued from previous page

H. narcissiflora, the most common deciduous type, is known for its daffodil-like flowers, which are borne in clusters of two to five atop 1- to 1½-foot stems.

H. speciosa is an evergreen West Indian species that produces umbels of up to 12 large flowers on 1- to 1½-foot stems in winter and early spring.

H. 'Sulphur Queen' is a hybrid of *H. narcissiflora* and produces sulphur-yellow flowers.

GROWING TIPS

Bloom time depends on species. Cultivation of most species is relatively simple; all that's required is fertile soil and adequate moisture. Both deciduous and evergreen types should be watered freely throughout the growing season. The evergreens do best when left undisturbed in their pots for several seasons; divide and repot only when necessary as growth begins in spring. Deciduous types are treated much like amaryllis hybrids: start them into growth in late spring. In the fall, after flowering is complete, dry the plants off and store them nearly dry in a cool place until it is time to restart them. Light requirements vary by type—evergreens do best in bright light shaded from hot sun, while their deciduous counterparts require full sun for best flowering.

Hymenocallis 'Sulphur Queen'

Wand Flower, Green Corn-lily

Wand flower is strangely beautiful in both color and habit: a spike of greenish blue, turquoise or variably colored flowers with dark central "eyes" is carried atop tall, thin reedy stems, to 3 feet. Flowers remain closed on cloudy days. The foliage is narrow, upright and stiff—contrasting with the flower stalk, which is flexible enough that it dances with the slightest breeze, giving the plant its common name, "wand flower."

CULTIVARS & RELATED SPECIES
I. dubia is, at 20 inches, more manageable in pots than *I. viridiflora*. It flowers in golden yellow to orange with a dark "eye," and is less fussy about wet feet than other members of this genus. *I. maculata* blooms in a handsome yellow or orange with an iridescent purple "eye," to 2 feet tall.

GROWING TIPS
Winter-early summer flowering. This is another winter-growing, summer-deciduous Cape species grown like *Gladiolus* (see page 78). It requires very careful watering: at bloom time too much water will rot this corm, and during summer it requires the usual dry rest. Support the flower spike, and guard against fungal diseases of the foliage.

T
E
N
D
E
R

Ixia hybrid

**T
E
N
D
E
R**

Kohleria

Kohleria is another genus in the African Violet family. Leaves and stems arise from scaly rhizomes and can reach a height of 6 inches to 4 feet, depending on the species. Kohlerias are similar to achimenes, except the foliage persists year round.

Hybrids are more commonly grown than the true species. Most of the species originate from Mexico and northern South America. The 1- to 2-inch flowers are borne singly in the axils of the leaves or in terminal clusters. Flower color ranges from white, pink and lavender to orange and red. Some hybrids are bicolored.

CULTIVARS & RELATED SPECIES

K. amabilis is a beautiful Columbian species with colorful leaf patterns in purple, brown and silver along the veins of the leaves. Flowers are usually pink. Hybrids generally do not have the strongly patterned foliage.

K. digitaliflora, a vigorous species, reaches 2 feet tall. Flowers are creamy white flushed with pink; hybrids produce pink, red or violet flowers.

GROWING TIPS

Spring-summer flowering. Start kohlerias anytime from February to May. Space the rhizomes 1 to 2 inches apart in a shallow flat or pan and cover with ½-inch of peat moss or vermiculite and water. Once the plants are 1 to 2 inches tall, transplant them individually into 4-inch pots and repot into successively larger pots as needed. Soil should be rich, moist and well-drained. Bright light shaded from hot afternoon sun is best. When blooming is finished, gradually dry off the rhizomes by reducing the amount of water, but provide enough water to keep the foliage from wilting.

Kohleria 'Princess'

Cape Cowslip

A spectacular plant in both leaf and flower, this South African species is extremely variable, with many named forms. Its two fleshy leaves are tulip-like and heavily blotched with maroon, which also speckles the thick flower stem. The flowers are tubular, in shades of yellow to golden orange, and hang from the stem like hyacinth flowers; they are usually marked with contrasting colors and have green, red or purple lips. The color combinations are often out-of-this-world.

CULTIVARS & RELATED SPECIES

L. aloides var. *aurea* has golden flowers on purple stalks and grows to 1 foot tall.

L. aloides var. *tricolor* has yellow and green flowers with reddish tips.

L. aloides var. *quadricolor* has red, yellow and green flowers with maroon tips.

L. contaminata is an unusual species—it has five to ten grass-like, mottled leaves per bulb; its flower is fragrant and white with maroon specks.

L. viridiflora is a beautiful species that flowers earlier than most in shades of greenish blue to turquoise, on short spikes. It requires good drainage.

GROWING TIPS

Winter-spring flowering. This Cape bulb grows in winter and goes dormant in hot weather. Grow in cool greenhouse conditions, in sun or light shade—avoid the scorching midday sun. Plant the bulbs in early autumn 2 to 3 inches deep, six to seven per 6-inch pot in a good potting mix cut with a third coarse sand. Water sparingly until growth is strong, then more freely, but don't let the soil get soggy. Fertilize lightly with a formula low in nitrogen such as 10-30-20. Allow the foliage to ripen in its own time, first reducing and then withholding water as leaves wither in late spring. Store dry in pots into summer, sort bulbs in August and replant in September or as soon as sprouting begins.

Lachenalia aloides

Blue Tulp

Linnaeus named this large South African genus of cormous plants after his wife's maiden name, Moraeus. Many of the moraeas now in cultivation are the progeny of seed distributed from the Kirstenbosch National Botanical Garden in an attempt to conserve endangered species; they are often beautiful, worthy of being grown as both horticultural and genetic treasures. Most *Moraea* flowers would be easily recognized by the novice as related to the European iris. There are a few evergreen species of moraeas, but most are winter-growing and summer-dormant like many South African bulbous plants.

CULTIVARS & RELATED SPECIES

M. aristata is endangered and beautiful, with white petals marked with blue watercolor-like accents.

M. villosa, the peacock moraea, grows 8 to 12 inches tall, sporting creamy to pale orange flowers with blue and green peacock-spot "eyes."

GROWING TIPS

Late fall-early spring flowering. Plant these easy-to-grow corms in the autumn in a well-drained soil, and then keep them in a cool and sunny spot. They aren't as fussy as some South African bulbous plants, and will tolerate indiscretions in both watering and fertilizing, making them a good choice for the novice.

Moraea polystachya

Guernsey-lily

This South African species is not as commonly grown as its numerous progeny; it possesses flowers of extra-ordinary beauty crowded atop a leaf-less stem. Pink and red forms predominate, and the undulating petals glisten and sparkle in sunlight. The stamens extend well beyond the petals on long filaments, giving the flower cluster a spidery appearance. Nerine leaves are few, long and strap-shaped, and emerge with the flower stem but elongate after flowering is complete in autumn.

CULTIVARS & RELATED SPECIES

N. fothergillii, a variant of *N. sarniensis*, has orange-scarlet flowers, prominent spidery filaments in fall, silvery gray leaves, and grows to 1½ to 2 feet tall.

N. masonorum is very dwarf—no more than 10 inches high—with dainty pink flowers and grassy leaves.

GROWING TIPS

Fall flowering. You may have difficulty getting your nerine to flower—this is not the best choice for the novice. Successful growers agree on a few points: *Do not* overwater, overfeed or overcrowd. Nerines naturally grow in very well-drained, nutrient-poor soil in full sun. Too much water or organic fertilizers can cause rotting; water only when dry, and if in doubt, don't water! Avoid nitrogen-rich fertilizers of any kind; they can suppress bloom for years. Nerines resent root disturbance; divide and repot with caution, making sure that the neck of the bulb is slightly above soil level. Even well-grown plants may skip blooming for a year or more. Mindful of these caveats, proceed: nerines possess such beauty that they continue to seduce the avid grower and collector.

T E N D E R

Nerine sarniensis

Oxalis, Wood Sorrel

The reputation of this South American and South African genus is tainted by the noxious weediness of some of its members, but a few others make well-behaved and charming potted bulbs. Oxalis flowers are five-petaled and open flat, with a cupped center; colors range from white through pink, red and yellow. Leaves are usually clover- or shamrock-shaped, sometimes needle-like, and most often grow in low, neat mounds.

CULTIVARS & RELATED SPECIES

O. tetraphylla 'Iron Cross' has cross-shaped brown blotches on it leaves.

O. massoniana, at 3 to 4 inches, is a dwarf species with soft-orange flowers and delicate foliage.

O. purpurea usually has pink flowers with a yellow eye, but can be variable; white and yellow forms exist. At 10 to 12 inches tall, it's great for pots.

O. regnellii is another species with wonderful foliage, green suffused with purple above, vivid purple beneath. Flowers pale pink to white.

GROWING TIPS

Flowering time varies with species. Plant the small bulbs about an inch deep, several per pot, in a well-drained mix in full sun. The most available species are almost always easy to grow: they prefer cool temperatures but are undemanding. Withhold water from the plants during dormancy, which is typically in winter. Pests and diseases are uncommon.

Oxalis regnellii

Pleione

Pleiones are a challenging group of orchids native to rich woodlands of Asia. The name *Pleione* refers to the mother of the Pleiades in Greek mythology. The "bulbs" of this genus are actually pseudobulbs—spherical, fleshy, hard stems adapted for water storage—a feature common in most orchid genera. However, unlike those of most other orchids, which last longer, pleione pseudobulbs persist for only one year and are replaced by new pseudobulbs annually.

CULTIVARS & RELATED SPECIES

P. bulbocodioides, from China and Taiwan, is the most widely grown of the genus. Flowering occurs as the foliage emerges in spring. Flowers are 2 to 2½ inches across; color ranges from deep to pale mauve and sometimes white. After flowering the foliage matures at less than 12 inches.

GROWING TIPS

Spring flowering. Pot the pseudobulbs in shallow bulb pans about 3 inches apart, with two-thirds visible above the soil line. Unlike most orchids, pleiones prefer a true soil mix that is well-drained and rich in organic matter. They thrive in bright light and high humidity.

Successful cultivation of pleiones depends greatly on temperature—especially cool night temperatures of 50° to 55° F. At higher temperatures, the plants will respire too quickly and burn out. Pleiones also require a dormancy in winter. At the end of the growing season, as the foliage begins to wither, reduce water. Store the new crop of pseudobulbs dry at 40° to 50° F and restart them in spring.

Pleione hybrid

Persian Buttercup

Ranunculus is a large genus of more than 400 species that occur throughout the temperate world, but few are cultivated. The name of the genus comes from the Latin "rana," or frog, referring to the fact that many species grow in moist to wet soils. The types grown as florists' crops are known as Persian or turban buttercups, and have large, usually double, brightly colored flowers up to 4 inches across, from white, pink and rose to yellow.

CULTIVARS & RELATED SPECIES

Bloomingdale hybrids are notable for their dwarf habit, reaching 8 to 10 inches in height with a 12- to 15-inch spread. Flowers are pink, red, white, yellow and tangerine.

GROWING TIPS

Winter-spring flowering. Cultivation of Persian buttercups can be quite challenging, but if you meet a few requirements you will increase your chances of success. First and foremost is temperature. Buttercups require cool temperatures (50° to 55° F) during the growing season, which extends from early fall into spring. If temperatures are higher, the plants will be spindly and burn out. The second critical factor is adequate drainage. The soil mix should be not only well drained but also rich in organic matter. What's more, during the growing season the plants require as much sun as possible.

In early fall, pot the tubers in shallow pans no more than 6 to 8 inches across and water sparingly until growth starts. As growth increases, water freely until flowering is finished and the foliage begins to wither. Store the tubers in a cool, dry place until fall.

'Tecolote' series hybrid

Florist's Gloxinia

Sinningia has been popular since Victorian times and long cultivated as "gloxinia," and the use of this erroneous common name seems unshakable. Bell-shaped, captivatingly large and colorful blooms crown the plant. The flowers of common hybrids have wide mouths and are held upright. The flowers of the wild forms of this Central and South American native are slipper-shaped and somewhat pendulous. They possess a quiet gracefulness and are charming in pots.

CULTIVARS & RELATED SPECIES
S. pusilla is a very dwarf thimble-sized species that is commonly evergreen and free-blooming, but requires near terrarium conditions.

GROWING TIPS
Summer blooming. Sinningia tubers are generally available late winter through spring. Remove all sprouts before potting: tiny insults to the minute leaves expand over time to notable flaws; the potted tuber will sprout anew, undamaged. Plant the tubers just below the soil surface in a light, rich mix. Water sparingly until growth is strong, then keep lightly, evenly moist. Removing all but one shoot is a common growing practice, resulting in fewer but larger flowers and leaves on a vigorous stem. Normal room temperatures are fine, and bright light without harsh sun is best. You may feed the plant frequently with a quarter-strength 10-30-20 fertilizer. When foliage ripens after bloom, withhold water. The tubers can remain potted unless pot-bound or in exhausted soil. Watch for signs of renewed growth, then resume watering.

TENDER

Sinningia speciosa

Harlequin Flower, Wand Flower

Sparaxis is easy to grow and is a knockout. The dramatic flowers of *Sparaxis tricolor*, which is very rare in the wild, have attracted the interest of breeders and many forms are offered in catalogs. The boldly colored flowers are streaked with contrasting colors and patterned with black markings and a bright yellow throat.

CULTIVARS & RELATED SPECIES

S. bulbifera is white to creamy yellow, grows to about 2 feet, and is easy to grow. Small bulbs form at each joint and leaf base.

S. elegans is a striking plant with intri-cate patterns of black with yellow flecks and creamy orange to buff outer petals arising from an iridescent purple throat.

GROWING TIPS

Spring flowering. Another South African cool-winter grower, *S. tricolor* presents no special problems. Good drainage, full sun, cool greenhouse temperatures and some support for the wiry flower stems should suffice. Plant about five bulbs per 6-inch pot, water freely while actively growing and fertilize very lightly. The plant is summer dormant; store it dry.

Sparaxis cultivar

Society Garlic

The introduction of a variegated form of *Tulbaghia,* with thin white leaf margins giving the plant a pinstriped appearance, has increased this plant's popularity and decorative possibilities. This South African native is a clump-forming rhizomatous plant that blooms for a prolonged period in spring and summer, with allium-like mauve flowers high above narrow strap-shaped leaves. The leaves emit a faint scent of garlic.

CULTIVARS & RELATED SPECIES
T. fragrans, pink agapanthus, is larger and coarser than *T. violacea,* with lavender-pink flowers in spring that are sweetly scented at night. It may bloom again in the fall.

GROWING TIPS
Summer flowering. *Tulbaghia* is very easy to grow. Mass the rhizomes in their container for better effect, and grow in a sunny position in average potting soil. Keep the soil moist but not wet, and make sure the plant gets good air circulation. Allow *Tulbaghia* to go a bit on the dry side in summer. It's evergreen indoors, and repotting or division is best accomplished in spring; feed it lightly in late spring. No serious pests.

Tulbaghia violacea 'Silver Lace'

T E N D E R

Winter Red Hot Poker

The common name attests to the resemblance of the flower spike to *Kniphofia*, but the plants are unrelated. The overall effect of the drooping, tubular rosy orange, green-tipped flowers is dramatic. The handsome foliage forms a rosette at the base of the flower stem, and the nearly evergreen plants are briefly deciduous in late summer. The flower spike follows fast upon the leaves and is long lasting, providing color from early winter well into spring. This South African native is highly recommended.

CULTIVARS & RELATED SPECIES

V. capensis, another of the handful of species in the genus, is from a more arid section of South Africa. Its leaves are bluer and stiffer and its flowers a purplish pink. It also blooms earlier, requires more sun and has a longer dormancy than *V. bracteata.*

Veltheimia bracteata

GROWING TIPS

Winter flowering. An excellent and easy container plant. Because the bulb is large and will produce offsets, choose a container that is large enough to accommodate its clumping for a few seasons. Plant with the top of the bulb just at the soil surface in a mix that provides good drainage. Grow in bright light but avoid hot sun. Provide even moisture, and a general-purpose granular or slow-release fertilizer for flowering pot plants. The only other requirement is a dry period during the brief summer dormancy.

Calla lily

Long a favorite of artists and florists, this flower is cosmopolitan in its appeal. The flower is the epitome of elegance: the flower spike or spadix is enveloped in the silken funnel formed by the spathe, or leaf. The large arrowhead-shaped leaves are held aloft by thick stems that clasp the base of the plant. Calla lily is native to South Africa's marshes where it grows to 6 feet. In cultivation the plant can grow to about 3 feet, still a commanding presence.

CULTIVARS & RELATED SPECIES

Z. albomaculata, compact at 2 feet, has a greenish white spathe with crimson blotches. Variegated foliage has translucent spots. Summer dormant.

Z. elliotiana has a beautiful yellow spathe, spotted leaves and grows to 2 feet. Summer blooming, winter dormant.

Z. rehmannii is another summer grower, in various shades of pink, with tapering unlobed leaves, generally less than 2 feet tall.

Zantedeschia rehmannii 'Superba'

GROWING TIPS

Moisture is the key to good growth. Callas like a very rich and moist potting mix and once growing respond to heavy feeding. Plant three rhizomes about 4 inches deep in a 12-inch pot. You can grow the plant warm or cool, in sun or partial shade. It may be briefly deciduous in summer if it's allowed to go dry— this is an opportunity to divide rhizomes if needed. Be on guard for bacterial rots, and remove affected parts. Thrips flourish on the plant's copious pollen.

Fairy-lily

T
E
N
D
E
R

An easy charmer for the windowsill, this dwarf bulb native to the American subtropics has lily-like pink flowers. For those with limited space, this plant is especially desirable. *Zephyranthes* are sometimes also called rain-lilies, because of their habit of bursting into flower when rain follows a dry period; this gives a hint as to how you should treat these bulbs in cultivation to force extra blooms.

CULTIVARS & RELATED SPECIES

Z. candida, an evergreen species, sports several flushes of crocus-like white flowers in the fall.

Z. flavissima is considered the best of the yellow *Zephyranthes;* it flowers for several months, with a peak in late summer. Requires very moist soil summer through fall.

Z. rosea, from Cuba, has lovely pink funnel-shaped flowers.

GROWING TIPS

Late-summer blooming. Plant *Zephyranthes* in a rich soil cut with some grit or sand, and make sure it gets good light. You can maintain it as an evergreen, but water it less in winter. During spring and summer, feed the plant with a 10-30-20 strength fertilizer.

Zephyranthes rosea

Ginger

Zingiber officinale, the common edible ginger, is the most familiar of a genus of nearly 100 different species native to Indo-Malaysia, Indonesia, eastern Asia and Australia. The genus gets its name from the Sanskrit word for horn.

Gingers have fleshy, rhizomatous rootstocks from which graceful, reed-like stems arise. Plant height varies from 1 to 12 feet, depending on the species, but less in containers. Unlike flowers of the similar hedychiums, or ginger-lilies, those of most true gingers are borne on stalks arising direct-ly from the soil. The flowers are clustered on cone-like spikes and surrounded by large bracts. Flower color ranges from pure white and pink to yellow, orange and red.

CULTIVARS & RELATED SPECIES

Z. spectabile, from Malaysia, is the largest species, growing to 6 feet (smaller in containers). Its yellow flowers are borne in 8- to 12-inch spikes surrounded by yellow to scarlet bracts. *Z. zerumbet*, among the most popular ornamentals, and its cultivar 'Darceyi' with strikingly variegated foliage, have white to yellow flowers surrounded by red bracts.

GROWING TIPS

Spring-summer blooming. Cultivation of most species is relatively simple: all that's required is fertile soil and adequate moisture. Water gingers freely throughout the growing season. Plants will tolerate a number of different exposures but need protection from hot afternoon sun. They require a period of dormancy in late fall, which you can initiate by gradually reducing water until the foliage withers. Resume watering in spring. Repotting and division are best done at this time.

Zingiber spectabile

T
E
N
D
E
R

101

FURTHER READING

Bulbs, vols. I & II
John E. Bryan
Timber Press, Portland, Oregon, 1989
The most comprehensive treatment of bulbs, with detailed information on all aspects of growing, as well as encyclope-dia-style entries on hundreds of species and their cultivars, color photos and reproductions of botanical illustrations.

Bulb Magic in Your Window
Ruth Marie Peters
William Morrow & Company, New York, 1954
This 42-year-old volume continues to be as helpful, clear, fun to read and accu-rate as when first published.

Bulbous Plants of South Africa: A Guide to Their Cultivation and Propagation
Niel Du Plessis and Graham Duncan
Tafelberg Publisher Ltd., Cape Town, South Africa, 1989
In addition to beautiful hand-painted illustrations of bulbs, this book briefly covers the exact habitat of each bulb, a history of its cultivation, and how to propagate.

Classic Bulbs
Katherine Whiteside
Villard Books, New York, 1991
This volume focuses on antique bulbs that can be grown indoors and out. It's sprinkled with lots of historical informa-tion about each bulb's travels and is illustrated with many good photos.

Holland Bulb Forcer's Guide
August De Hertogh
Department of Horticultural Science, North Carolina State University; Available from Ball Publishing, 708-208-9080.
Used in the commercial bulb forcing world as a guide to scheduling crop pro-duction, this technical volume lists spe-cific cultivars and their chilling require-ments.

The Indoor Potted Bulb
Rob Proctor
Simon & Schuster, New York, 1993
This book will ease you into indoor bulb cultivation with its friendly, inviting approach, easy-to-follow growing guid-ance and photos of bulbs in groupings and interesting containers.

The Royal Horticultural Society Manual of Bulbs
John E. Bryan, editor
Timber Press, Portland, Oregon, 1995
This comprehensive, well organized vol-ume has a glossary and entries covering practically every species and cultivar of bulb, with excellent line drawings of most plants, but is most useful to a tech-nically versed audience.

Some bulbs are imperiled by collectors, private and commercial, who dig them up from the wild. Buy bulbs only from nurseries that propagate the bulbs they sell!

ANTONELLI BROTHERS, INC.
2545 Capitola Road
Santa Cruz, CA 95062
(408) 475-5222
Catalog, $1

B&D LILIES
330 P Street
Port Townsend, WA 98368
(360) 385-1738
Catalog, $3

BOTANICAL SOCIETY OF SOUTH AFRICA
Kirstenbosch, Claremont 7735
Republic of South Africa
Write for membership information; seeds and bulbs are available to members only

THE DAFFODIL MART
7463 Heath Trail
Gloucester, VA 23061
(800) ALL-BULB
Free Catalog

DUTCH GARDENS
P.O. Box 200
Adelphia, NJ 07710-0200

(800) 818-3861
Free Catalog

FAIRYLAND BEGONIA GARDEN
1100 Griffith Road
McKinleyville, CA 95519
(707) 839-3034
Catalog, 50¢

GAINESVILLE TREE FARM & LANDSCAPE PLANTS
3714 NW 39th Avenue
Gainesville, FL 32606
(904) 372-7325
Catalog free with stamped self-addressed envelope

KELLY'S PLANT WORLD
10266 East Princeton
Sanger, CA 93657
(209) 292-3505
Catalog, $1

LOGEE'S GREENHOUSES
141 North Street
Danielson, CT 06239
(203) 774-8038
Catalog, $3

MCCLURE & ZIMMERMAN
P.O. Box 368
108 W. Winnebago
Friesland, WI 53935
(414) 326-4220
Free Catalog

MESSELAAR BULB CO.
P.O. Box 269
Ipswich, MA 01938
(508) 356-3737
Free Catalog

**GRANT E. MITSCH NOVELTY
DAFFODILS**
P.O. Box 218
Hubbard, OR 97032
(503) 651-2742
Catalog, $3

OLD HOUSE GARDENS
536 Third Street
Ann Arbor, MI 48103-4957
Catalog, $2

OREGON TRAIL DAFFODILS
41905 S.E. Louden
Corbett, OR 97019
(503) 695-5513
Free Catalog

PARK SEED CO.
Cokesbury Road
Greenwood, SC 29647-0001
(803) 223-7333
Free Catalog

RUST-EN-VREDE NURSERY
P.O. Box 753
Brackenfell 7560
Republic of South Africa

JOHN SCHEEPERS INC.
P.O. Box 700
Bantam, CT 06750
(203) 567-0838
Free Catalog

VAN BOURGONDIEN BROS.
P.O. Box 1000
245 Farmingdale Road, Rte. 109
Babylon, NY 11702-0598
(800) 622-9997
Free Catalog

VAN ENGELEN, INC.
Stillbrook Farm
313 Maple Street
Litchfield, CT 06759
(203) 567-8734
Free Catalog

THE WAUSHARA GARDENS
N5491 Fifth Drive
Plainfield, WI 54966
(715) 335-4462
Free Catalog

WHITE FLOWER FARM
P.O. Box 50
Litchfield, CT 06759-0050
(800) 503-9624
Free Catalog

CONTRIBUTORS

SCOTT CANNING is the gardener in charge of the Warm Temperate House, Trail of Evolution and Monocot Terrace in the Brooklyn Botanic Garden's Steinhardt Conservatory. He wrote the sections on *Agapanthus, Babiana, Begonia, Caladium, Clivia, Cyrtanthus, Eucharis, Freesia, Gladiolus, Haemanthus, Homeria, Ixia, Lachenalia, Moraea, Nerine, Oxalis, Sinningia, Sparaxis, Tulbaghia, Veltheimia, Zantedeschia* and *Zephyranthes* in the Encyclopedia of Tender Bulbs for Indoors.

STEVEN E. CLEMANTS is a botanist and coordinator of the Brooklyn Botanic Garden's New York Metropolitan Flora Project, a multi-year effort to document the plant diversity in all counties within a 50-mile radius of New York City. He teaches classes on the morphology of geophytes and other plants.

MARK FISHER is foreman of the Brooklyn Botanic Garden's Steinhardt Conservatory. He wrote the chapter on growing hardy bulbs indoors, as well as all the entries in the Encyclopedia of Hardy Bulbs for Indoors. Mark forces all the bulbs for BBG's annual Spring Flower Show.

ROBERT M. HAYS is co-editor of this handbook. Propagator at the Brooklyn Botanic Garden, he is also coordinator of the Garden's Signature Seeds and Plants programs—and unofficial "Canna King" of the Western Hemisphere. Bob wrote the encyclopedia entries for the following tender bulbs: *Achimenes, Alpinia, Boophane, Crinum, Curcuma, Cyclamen, Eucrosia, Globba, Hedychium, Hippeastrum, Hymenocallis, Kohleria, Pleione, Ranunculus* and *Zingiber*.

JANET MARINELLI, co-editor of this handbook, is director of publishing at the Brooklyn Botanic Garden and the author of two books that explore the frontiers of ecological design: *The Naturally Elegant Home* and *Your Natural Home*, both published by Little, Brown and Company. She is also editor of two BBG handbooks: *The Environmental Gardener* and *Going Native: Biodiversity in Our Own Backyards*. She grows antique bulbs indoors and out at her Victorian Brooklyn brownstone.

TOVAH MARTIN is the author of several books, including *Tasha Tudor's Garden, Well-Clad Windowsills* and *The Essence of Paradise: Fragrant Plants for Indoor Gardens*. She is the garden editor of *Victoria* magazine and a horticulturist at White Flower Farm. Her greenhouse in Roxbury, Connecticut, is filled to the brim with bulbs both hardy and tender.

ILLUSTRATION CREDITS

DRAWINGS BY **STEVE BUCHANAN**

PHOTOS:
COVER AND PAGES 7, 14, 15 TOP AND BOTTOM, 16, 21, 24 (ALL), 32 35, 36, 38, 42, 43, 45, 46, 47, 48, 49, 50, 54 LEFT AND RIGHT, 55 RIGHT, 56 LEFT, 62, 65, 68, 69, 72, 73, 74, 75, 78, 79, 80, 81, 82, 86, 88, 91, 92, 93, 94, 97, 99 AND 101 BY **CHARLES MARDEN FITCH**

PAGES 1, 8, 19, 20, 23, 25, 27, 44, 57, 59 AND 86 BY **ROB PROCTOR**

PAGES 4, 13, 28, 58 LEFT AND RIGHT, 84, 90, 98 AND 108 BY **CHRISTINE DOUGLAS**

PAGES 10 AND 11 BY **ROBERT ORNDUFF**

PAGES 12, 30, 31, 37, 39, 41, 53 AND 96 BY **THE NETHERLANDS FLOWERBULB INFORMATION CENTER**

PAGES 26, 33, 34, 40 AND 100 BY **BRENT HEATH**

PAGE 55 LEFT BY **JUDYWHITE**

PAGES 56 RIGHT, 66 AND 67 BY **CHARLES O. CRESSON**

PAGES 63 AND 70 BY **JERRY PAVIA**

PAGES 64, 71 AND 77 BY **PETER NELSON**

PAGE 76 BY **BETSY KISSAM**

PAGE 85 BY **CATHY WILKINSON BARASH**

PAGE 87 BY **ANITA SABARESE**

PAGES 89 AND 95 BY **PAMELA HARPER**

INDEX

Gardening Books for the Next Century

Don't miss any of the gardening books in Brooklyn Botanic Garden's 21st-Century Gardening Series! Published four times a year, these acclaimed books explore the frontiers of ecological gardening—offering practical, step-by-step tips on creating environmentally sensitive and beautiful gardens for the 1990s and the new century. Your subscription to BBG's 21st-Century Gardening Series is free with Brooklyn Botanic Garden membership.

To become a member, please call (718) 622-4433, ext. 265. Or photocopy this form, complete and return to: Membership Department, Brooklyn Botanic Garden, 1000 Washington Avenue, Brooklyn, NY 11225-1099.

SUBSCRIPTIONS

Your name ....

Address ....

City/State/Zip ....Phone ....

AMOUNT

☐ Yes, I want to subscribe to the 21st-Century Gardening Series (4 quarterly volumes) by becoming a member of the Brooklyn Botanic Garden:

☐ $35 (Subscriber)   ☐ $125 (Signature Member)

☐ $50 (Partner)   ☐ $300 (Benefactor)   ....

☐ Enclosed is my tax-deductible contribution to the Brooklyn Botanic Garden.   ....

TOTAL   ....

Form of payment: ☐ Check enclosed ☐ Visa ☐ Mastercard

Credit card# ....Exp ....

Signature ....

FOR INFORMATION ON ORDERING ANY OF THE FOLLOWING BACK TITLES, PLEASE WRITE THE BROOKLYN BOTANIC GARDEN AT THE ABOVE ADDRESS OR CALL (718) 622-4433, EXT. 274.

American Cottage Gardening
Annuals: A Gardener's Guide
Bonsai: Special Techniques
Butterfly Gardens
Culinary Herbs
Easy-care Roses
The Environmental Gardener
Ferns
Garden Photography
The Gardener's World of Bulbs
Gardening for Fragrance
Gardening in the Shade
Gardening with Wildflowers
 & Native Plants

Going Native: Biodiversity
 in Our Own Backyards
Greenhouses & Garden Rooms
Growing Fruits
Herbs & Cooking
Herbs & Their Ornamental Uses
Hollies: A Gardener's Guide
Indoor Bonsai
Japanese Gardens
Native Perennials
The Natural Lawn & Alternatives
Natural Insect Control
A New Look at Vegetables
A New Look at Houseplants
Orchids for the Home

 & Greenhouse
Ornamental Grasses
Perennials: A Gardener's Guide
Pruning Techniques
Roses
Salad Gardens
Shrubs: The New Glamour Plants
Soils
The Town & City Gardener
Trees: A Gardener's Guide
Water Gardening
The Winter Garden
Woodland Gardens: Shade
 Gets Chic